# GREEN AND WHITE ARMY
## THE NORTHERN IRELAND FANS

Ivan Martin

Photographs by Gary Hancock

Appletree Press

*For Colin who fights the good fight every day*

*and is an inspiration to us all.*

First published in 2008 by
Appletree Press Ltd
The Old Potato Station
14 Howard Street South
Belfast BT7 1AP

Tel: +44 (0) 28 90 24 30 74
Fax: +44 (0) 28 90 24 67 56
Website: www.appletree.ie
Email: reception@appletree.ie

A catalogue record for this book is available from the British Library.

**Green and White Army – The Northern Ireland Fans**

ISBN: 978 1 84758 088 7

Desk & Marketing Editor: Jean Brown
Copy Editor: Jim Black
Designer: Kevin Hippsley
Production Manager: Paul McAvoy

9 8 7 6 5 4 3 2 1

AP3536

# CONTENTS

# *Foreword* by *Howard Wells*

The EURO 2008 Qualifying Campaign began on a very sunny Saturday on 2 September 2006. Hopes were high and the pre-match lunch with the officials from Iceland was a joyous occasion. There was a good deal of banter around the game and we all set out for Windsor Park probably thinking the result was a forgone conclusion. The 0-3 defeat was a shock to the system as Eider Gudjohnnson virtually 'ran' the match for 45 minutes and by half time it was as good as over.

In typical Northern Ireland style though four days later, the team stepped up to the mark against Spain. An uncanny hat-trick from David Healy, coupled with an amazing debut by Jonny Evans, who played Liverpool's Torres out of the game, was enough to bring the team back from the dead having twice been behind in the match, to run out 3-2 winners.

The roller coaster that manager Lawrie Sanchez had predicted was to continue. When he stood down to take over at Fulham midway through the campaign, with Northern Ireland at the top of the group with 13 points, having by then beaten not only Spain, but Sweden and Latvia at home, drawn in Denmark and recorded a rare away win in Liechtenstein, hopes were high.

We will never know what might have been had Lawrie remained with the team. That is not to take credit away from Nigel Worthington, but to step in half way through a campaign was always going to be a tall order, especially with four of the final six matches to be played away. Lawrie must since have asked himself whether he might have done things differently, because there is no doubt that his departure caused an uncertainty which might have been greater had Nigel not stepped up to accept the challenge so positively and in completing the double against Liechtenstein in his first match, the wheels were rolling again. The ensuing disappointments in Latvia and Iceland in the double header when both defeats 0-1 and 1-2 were from own goals, was probably more to do with poor long term planning on the part of the IFA, than poor performances. Being 'on the road' for nine days proved difficult for the new coaching team and the players.

But then again a great 1-1 draw in Sweden with Kyle Lafferty scoring a tremendous equaliser raised expectations. This was compounded on a wet night at Windsor Park on a quagmire of a pitch when two goals from Warren Feeney and David Healy undid Denmark and took the campaign to the wire with the chance of qualification still a possibility up to the final group match against Spain in Gran Canaria.

That the chances of qualification remained until that match in Spain was a major factor throughout in encouraging the hordes of the Green and White Army who helped keep the dream alive and their contribution to the overall performance must not be under-estimated. Had we all thought after that depressing reversal against Iceland that along with Scotland and England we would still be in with a real chance of qualifying right up to the end of the competition we would probably have been delighted. The truth is we could have qualified had we had a couple of breaks, but that is football. In the process of moving forward, firstly under Lawrie Sanchez and now under Nigel Worthington, we have set new standards and raised our sights. The challenge now is to keep the momentum going, and to maintain that much-appreciated support which has become synonymous with the team.

Howard JC Wells
Irish Football Association

# THE IFA

*Nigel Worthington gives instructions to Jonny Evans in the away Iceland game.*

# Nigel Worthington

Throughout his career Nigel Worthington has been a winner. As a player his no-nonsense style and will to win endeared him to the Northern Ireland faithful. Home or away, he always turned up. No sudden groin strains, hamstring tugs or other 'convenient' injuries for Nigel, who won 66 caps in a thirteen-year spell as a Northern Ireland stalwart.

Since becoming boss of the national team in June 2007, the goodwill Worthington got from the fans in his playing days has transferred to an appreciation of his managerial style.

He is grateful for the unwavering support of the fans. They were shell-shocked by the way they and the team were ditched by Lawrie Sanchez, who exited for a short and unsuccessful spell at Fulham.

Worthington came in and immediately calmed everything down. His commitment to the Northern Ireland cause was the tonic the fans needed. He further underlined that by signing a contract for the 2010 World Cup qualifying campaign which included an assurance that he would not quit mid-term. He would see the job through.

"What can I say about the Northern Ireland fans?" asks Nigel. "Their support – home and away – has been both phenomenal and fanatical. It is great for the players and for me as a manager, and I am very grateful for it."

Worthington has moved the side away from the route-one, Wimbledon style of the former manager to a more subtle game.

"I make no apology for the fact that I like the team to pass it around," explains Nigel. "A high tempo game, with good passing and an end product is what I am looking for. The fans appreciate that, and the best example of it in my time as manager was the first half of the Georgia game, which had all of that and produced three goals.

"The way the fans got behind the team enabled that to happen. The role of the supporters has always been to lift the spirits of the team. They have consistently done that. They are also a jovial bunch who go out to enjoy themselves and also behave. That is important, as it reflects badly on the image of Northern Ireland, especially abroad, if there is any trouble. Happily that does not happen at our games.

"There is an undoubted bond between the team and the supporters. The Northern Ireland players appreciate the supporters, and know that no matter how remote the venue we play at the Green and White Army will be there, making themselves heard."

# Derek McKinley

Derek McKinley has been the Northern Ireland kit man since November 1981. His career began with the highs of the Bingham era, two World Cups and a sprinkling of some of the greats of Northern Ireland football. He also remembers how those teams used to mix freely with the fans who would turn up at their hotel. It was one big, happy family.

"Billy encouraged the rapport between the players and the travelling fans," explains Derek. "But the fans themselves were amazing. I remember the night we beat Spain 1-0 to qualify for the quarter final. The Northern Ireland fans out-shouted, out-sung and outshone the Spaniards.

"But they were always made welcome wherever they went. The local beer was 'San Miguel', and shortly after the fans arrived in Valencia for the opening game they went to the pubs. The staff were a wee bit reticent with them at first, especially as they kept ordering 'wee Sammies', which confused the barmen. But they soon realised the lads meant 'San Miguel' and were well behaved. After that the Northern Ireland fans were welcomed everywhere by the staff who would shout 'Wee Sammies. Wee Sammies'."

Derek was there through the bad times and the low point of going 1298 minutes without Northern Ireland scoring a goal. But that is all history now, and since beating England the team has gone from strength to strength.

"Everywhere you go in Northern Ireland these days you see people wearing Northern Ireland tops. The new songs are great, with the one about Steven Davis my favourite. Sometimes when I look up to the Alex Russell stand I would love to be in there doing the 'bouncy' with them all. The problem is that I probably could not get in.

"I remember the days when we used to travel with sixty or seventy fans, tops. Now it's 4000 or more. In Liechtenstein the fans took over the square before the match. During the game you would have thought we were the home side. That level of support has been reflected elsewhere, which is a great incentive for the players. I reckon we could now fill a 25,000 to 30,000 all-seater stadium without any problem."

# The Players on the Fans

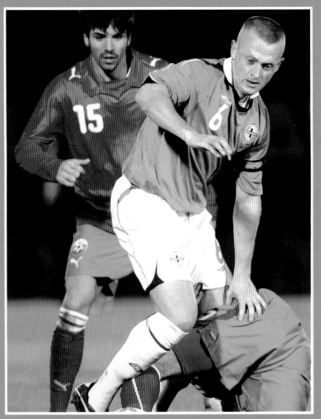

*Sammy Clingan.*

*Warren Feeney.*

The Northern Ireland supporters are as fanatical as any set of international fans in the world. It is easy to sing when you are winning, but at times there has been very little on offer in terms of victories.

But when it comes to making the most of adversity the Green and White Army has no equal. The best example of this came when the team went 1298 minutes without scoring a goal. That was the total number of minutes between Steve Lomas scoring against Poland in February 2002 and David Healy ending the famine at Windsor Park in a 4-1 defeat by Norway in February 2004.

*David Healy fights for control during the away Iceland match*

It brought a premature end to Sammy McIlroy's reign as national manager. "The monkey round our neck", as he was prone to refer to the goal drought, saw him opt for pastures new at Stockport County.

The fans reacted to Northern Ireland creating a new world record for the longest period between goals by getting special commemorative T-shirts printed.

The ability to react like that in adversity leaves the Northern Ireland fans a cut above the rest. Nigel Worthington has described them as "part of our team" and Sammy Clingan freely acknowledges their role in the team's upward spiral in recent times.

"The fans have been a huge factor in making Windsor Park such a fortress again. Absolutely superb," stated Sammy. "The noise and atmosphere they create at home is amazing: it makes teams fear coming to Belfast. It also gave the players belief that they could beat anybody at home and that showed, the way we came from behind against Spain, Sweden and Denmark. The fans also follow us in large numbers to away games as well, and after the final match against Spain all the players went over to applaud them, to show their appreciation."

Like all Northern Ireland players Warren Feeney is quick to pay tribute to the fantastic atmosphere created by the fans throughout the Euro 2008 campaign, especially at Windsor Park.

*From left: Michael Duff, Maik Taylor and Chris Baird.*

"The noise the fans make is incredible. You would think there was 30,000 or 40,000 in the stadium. That is probably why teams fear coming to Windsor and why we have such a good home record against the top countries," says the striker, who is the third generation of his family to wear the famous green jersey. "In my opinion Northern Ireland should continue to play at Windsor Park, with the South and Railway Stands being re-developed, rather than move to a new stadium."

Chris Baird also sees Windsor Park as a genuine asset to the team, and feels opposition sides could well feel intimidated by the cauldron of noise that awaits them at the home of international football in Northern Ireland.

"The support over the past few years has been unbelievable. A full house at Windsor makes as much noise as 30,000 fans and that type of support makes you want to work even harder on the pitch. Sometimes in a break in play during games at Windsor the players just look around at the whole ground doing the 'bouncy' and it's an absolutely amazing sight. Support like that really does make a difference," says the Rasharkin man.

*Stephen Craigan in action against Liechtenstein.*

Rugged defender Stephen Craigan was delighted when the fans won their award in 2006. He feels their ability to get to the most out-of-the-way places, coupled with the noise they make when they get there, was reason enough for them to be honoured.

"It was great for our fans and they deserved this success. It is amazing to think that for a country of our size that we can attract two to three thousand supporters to away games. The vocal support of the fans, home and away, really does spur us on and long may it continue."

*Fred Barber (Goalkeeping Coach) left and Glynn Snodin (Assistant Manager).*

Two men who are recent arrivals on the Northern Ireland scene are Fred Barber and Glynn Snodin. They joined the set-up when Nigel Worthington took over as manager, and quickly came to appreciate the special nature of the Green and White Army.

"The fans are absolutely superb. I'm really amazed by the noise they generate at Windsor Park," observes Snodin. "The supporters also follow us in large numbers abroad, and I can tell you it's certainly appreciated by both the players and the management."

Barber admits that the reputation of the fans goes before them. He was already aware of the excellent reputation of the Northern Ireland supporters prior to his appointment in June 2007.

"I had heard the Northern Ireland fans really got behind their team, although I didn't realise how special they were until I experienced the atmosphere at Windsor Park first-hand," explains the goalkeeping coach.

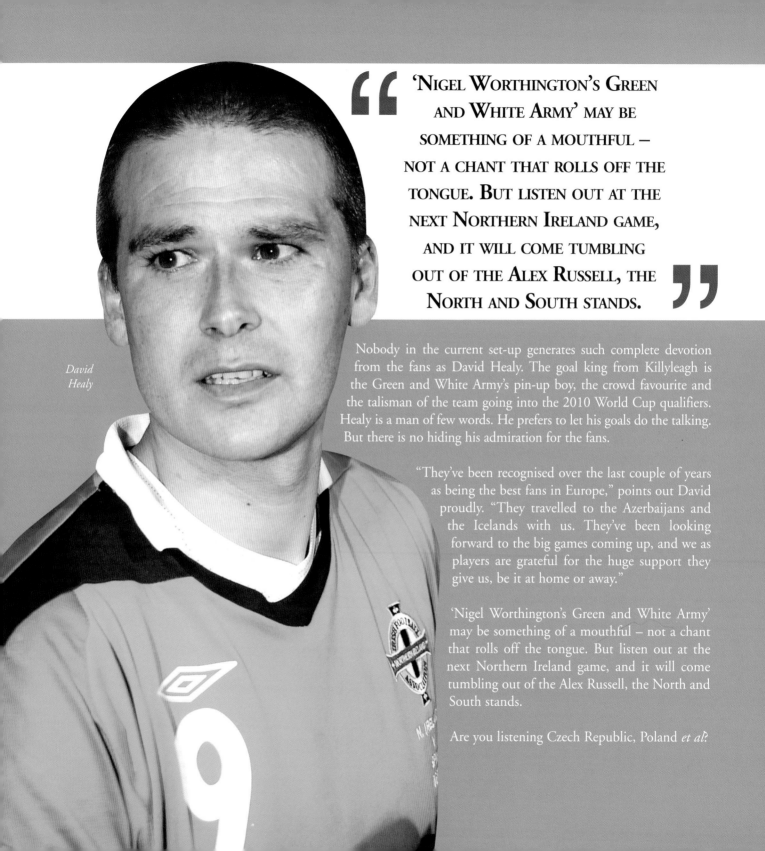

> **'NIGEL WORTHINGTON'S GREEN AND WHITE ARMY' MAY BE SOMETHING OF A MOUTHFUL — NOT A CHANT THAT ROLLS OFF THE TONGUE. BUT LISTEN OUT AT THE NEXT NORTHERN IRELAND GAME, AND IT WILL COME TUMBLING OUT OF THE ALEX RUSSELL, THE NORTH AND SOUTH STANDS.**

*David Healy*

Nobody in the current set-up generates such complete devotion from the fans as David Healy. The goal king from Killyleagh is the Green and White Army's pin-up boy, the crowd favourite and the talisman of the team going into the 2010 World Cup qualifiers. Healy is a man of few words. He prefers to let his goals do the talking. But there is no hiding his admiration for the fans.

"They've been recognised over the last couple of years as being the best fans in Europe," points out David proudly. "They travelled to the Azerbaijans and the Icelands with us. They've been looking forward to the big games coming up, and we as players are grateful for the huge support they give us, be it at home or away."

'Nigel Worthington's Green and White Army' may be something of a mouthful – not a chant that rolls off the tongue. But listen out at the next Northern Ireland game, and it will come tumbling out of the Alex Russell, the North and South stands.

Are you listening Czech Republic, Poland *et al*?

# Jim Boyce

Nobody has a better word for the Northern Ireland supporters than Jim Boyce. The former President of the IFA built up a special relationship with the Green and White Army during his time in the top job, but it was not always sweetness and light.

"There was a time five or six years ago when some of the chants at Windsor Park disgusted me," admits Jim. "I was not alone either. Dignitaries were becoming reticent about attending games, and people from both sides of the local community were writing to me saying they would not be back.

"That was not a nice situation and obviously something had to be done. So when a meeting was set up in the Wellington Park Hotel I agreed to go along and meet members of the Amalgamation. Jackie Fullerton chaired the discussion, and I was given a rough ride at the start. The fans were very hostile, and a lot of nonsense was being bandied about, that I had tried to get the national anthem banned before games, and had tried to prevent people with Ulster flags being admitted to the ground."

"In those days we had about 5000 fans attending games, and it was starting to dwindle. About 350 of them turned up at the meeting, which ended with me saying that things were in their hands. 'I can't change this but you can,' I told them. 'But it has to stop, because it is reflecting badly on our country and our national game.'

"They pledged that they would endeavour to change things but pointed out, quite reasonably, that it would take time. We shook hands, and some of the guys who had

*Jim makes a presentation to Aaron Hughes on his 50th cap.*

a very low opinion of me before the meeting began also shook my hand, which was pleasing.

"Things took off after that, and the actions of a few were no longer allowed to spoil things for the majority. That was all down to the supporters' actions. They have now turned Windsor Park into somewhere anyone could go. There are no obscenities, which have been replaced by a fun, family atmosphere. That is down to the supporters, and that is why I was delighted when they got the award from UEFA and the city of Brussels. It was thoroughly deserved.

"Since that meeting I mentioned there has been a real sea change. Windsor now sells out every time Northern

*IFA Life President Jim Boyce celebrates in Denmark.*

Ireland play, and had we a larger stadium we could undoubtedly sell a lot more tickets. Michael Boyd, the IFA's Head of Community Relations, has also done great work and has the respect and trust of the supporters. Like myself he has built up a tremendous rapport with them.

"I remember going down to salute them after that terrific draw in Denmark in November 2006. It was an emotional night, and after the game I just wanted to go onto the pitch to congratulate the team and the fans who were terrific throughout.

"The fans gave me a Northern Ireland scarf and a Viking hat and somebody snapped it. The rest as they say is history, because the next day the photograph was all over the place. It now has pride of place in my home. A lasting memory of a wonderful night, brought about by the generosity of spirit of those Northern Ireland fans."

*Northern Ireland fans celebrate after the draw in Copenhagen, Denmark.*

# Geoff Wilson

In less than three years since joining the IFA from BT Geoff Wilson has seen the Association move from being an under-achieving commercial entity to a flourishing operation. He is quick to acknowledge the encouragement and support he has received from Howard Wells and his own marketing team.

"It quickly became clear to me that we needed to develop the IFA brand. Fans said we didn't talk to them and sponsors were not being managed properly. We have addressed all those issues. There is now a great rapport with the fans as Michael [Boyd] has indicated elsewhere in this book and that is crucial.

"We need to be close to them to make the IFA a success. We need to listen to them. It is all about getting to know your customers and showing them they are important to you. We consulted them, for example, on the new strip which came out for the current World Cup qualifying campaign. Our strap line is 'IFA Bringing Communities Together' and we are committed to that."

One of the most visible signs of the rekindling of interest in the Northern Ireland team has been the number of jerseys that are being worn by people of all ages. They now seem to be up there with the Manchester Uniteds and Liverpools of this world. The stats bear this out.

"In our last World Cup campaign we sold 15,000 home shirts – during the qualifiers for Euro 2008 that increased to 65,000. We have other schemes which the fans can join in with, like our official supporters' scheme which costs just £40 per campaign. It brings everything from regular newsletters to priority ticketing for away games, access to youth and Under-21 games free and 10 per cent off goods bought directly from the IFA."

The IFA shop was launched in March 2006 and has expanded its range of goods way beyond basic kit and has quadrupled its turnover in the past year. A scheme for the junior supporters has also been developed, as has the IFA website. Before the launch of the new site in November 2005 it was getting 20,000 unique users per month: that has now risen to 90,000 every month.

Sponsors now meet with the Association on a regular basis and the revenue from it has doubled in the past year.

"Things have improved but there is still work to do. But at least we are going in the right direction," reveals Geoff.

# Magazine

Another marketing tool of the 21st century and the PR savvy Irish Football Association is the quarterly magazine. *NI Football* produced by Profile Publishing is a 58-page glossy magazine which covers both domestic and international football in Northern Ireland.

"We launched *Total Football* during the 2001-02 season," recalled Jason Andrews, the publishing manager at Profile. "It filled a vacuum at that time.

"In 2006, after a meeting with the IFA Head of Marketing and Communications Manager Geoff Wilson we began to publish *NI Football*, which was to become their official magazine, and was to be distributed free to all members of the then newly established Official Northern Ireland Supporters scheme. The publication is a good vehicle for the IFA to get across to the general public the work that is been carried out by the organisation behind the scenes.

"It also includes excellent coverage of domestic football in the province, regular interviews with Irish League and international players, and also sections profiling individual supporters and Northern Ireland Supporters' clubs."

# The Women's Game

Women's football in Northern Ireland is on the up and up. The interest in the game at grass roots level is immense, and that is starting to be reflected further up the ladder with a structure that goes right to the senior international team.

Sara Booth plays for that team but she has also worked full-time in the development of the women's game in Northern Ireland since 2002.

"In the early days Ian Stewart and Cheryl Lamont worked with me, and it was entirely different back then. In those days we got hand-me-down kit from the men. My mum still has photographs of me wearing jerseys that were down over my knuckles. Once I even got shorts which had chewing gum embedded in the pocket that just refused to shift.

"I remember one tournament where I managed to secure some funding from the Sports Council's Athletes Support Scheme. The IFA agreed to let us compete and kick-start the senior team again, after it had been allowed to lapse. The girls who went to that tournament had to stump up £150 of their own money, from memory. They also got involved in other fund-raising activities.

"Now it is very different. These days, the current senior squad wear the same playing and training kit as the men's teams. We stay in the same hotels, use the same training facilities and travel is organised by the IFA. We are totally integrated into the IFA structure, and results are starting to reflect that."

In 2005 Alfie Wylie was introduced to the women's set-up. His vast experience as a coach brought a new urgency to the Northern Ireland senior team.

"Sara was already there," explains Alfie. "What was needed was a structure from grassroots right through the schools to the senior squad. We worked on that which was vital, because many of the girls had nowhere to play once they left school. So the Under 17s and Under 19s were vitally important."

In the year Wylie was appointed the Northern Ireland Women's team beat both Kazakhstan and Slovakia in World Cup qualifying games. The second of these victories came rather appropriately, on the day the IFA had a special dinner in Belfast's City Hall to celebrate the 125th anniversary of its formation.

The following year the women's team was fourth seed in a four-team mini group for the European championships. They lost 1-0 to favourites Turkey, but had more morale-boosting success in the other games.

Ashley Hutton became the first Northern Ireland female player to score a hat trick on foreign soil, in a 4-0 victory over Georgia. Her feat was made even more special by the fact that all her three goals were headers. Not to be outdone Sarah McFadden bagged a hat trick in the final game, which saw pre-match favourites Croatia humbled 5-1.

The next target for the women is the 2009 World Cup. They are in a difficult group with England, Spain, Czech Republic and Belarus. It has been tough going, but they are getting there and hopefully will become one of Europe's Top 20 in coming years.

Undoubtedly though things are moving in the right direction. One of the reasons for this is the infrastructure that has been built up from grassroots level through the schools and on to the Under 17 and Under 19 teams, and ultimately senior level.

"Competition is the lifeblood of any sport," ventures Wylie who has been the IFA's supremo of the women's game since 2005. "We now have an excellence programme throughout

*Sara Booth with Kimberley Turner pictured at 'First Kicks' – a grassroots scheme for girls aged 4 – 11.*

the counties. Systems are in place in the schools and they can avail of professional coaching. The girls who come through that system now have the incentive to go on right through to the senior team. Fitness levels are good, results are starting to improve and the senior team has benefited from a batch of players from the successful Under 19 side graduating to it."

The IFA have invested a lot of time, effort and money into the grassroots game. The success of that policy has been reflected in several different areas, with women's football being a prime example. But at present the women's game is crying out for more people working in it who can deal with the explosion of interest around the country. At primary and post-primary level there are many schools who would like to compete in district leagues. The problem is a lack of numbers in both coaching and administration to move things on to the next level.

The IFA can only do so much. However in these health-conscious days when government warnings about increasing levels of obesity are frequently to be heard, perhaps some joint funding from the departments of education and health might be a smart idea. Food for thought...

# The IFA Disability Football Project

Special Needs was one area of football which had been neglected in Northern Ireland until the 1990s. This situation, it must be said, tended to mirror things in many other countries.

Then in 1996 the Irish Football Association with the support of Disability Sports Northern Ireland and The Sports Council for Northern Ireland, appointed Shane Maguire as Development Officer for Disability Football. The initial stage of work in this area was within Special Education, and predominately the area of Learning Disability. Structured coaching sessions were introduced into the Special Schools: a positive reaction ensued which allowed a good relationship to develop, with a subsequent increase in demand.

Like any type of sport, the natural progression from participation of this nature is to form competitive opportunities. The Special Schools FA Cup was created in 1999 by the new Development Officer, Lee Carroll. This involved playoffs in each Education and Library Board, with the regional winners progressing onto the national finals.

Participant numbers were also on the rise and to assist with the provision of this coaching service, Lee introduced a Disability Specific Coaching Course that gave coaches and teachers examples of Good Practice when working with players with a Learning Disability.

Lee also introduced a Representative strand to the Disability Project, forming a Learning Disability National side in 2002. This Squad would finish in seventh place in

*Aaron Hughes with pupils of Sperrinview Special School.*

the 2003 European Championships in Portugal. A strong performance pathway was now forming in Learning Disability in Football Ireland, from participation in Schools to pulling on the Green Jersey for Northern Ireland in a major Championship.

*Belfast Deaf United.*

There was a desire from the Association to mirror this development in Learning Disability within the areas of Physical Disability and Sensory Impairment. When Lee moved into Grassroots Football within the Association in 2003, Alan Crooks was appointed and a three-year Disability Football Development Strategy was written to do just that.

This strategy had five key components: to create and develop strong working relationships with the key players in the Disability Sector; to increase the number of disabled performers involved in football activities; to improve and increase the number of competitive opportunities for all disabled groups; to develop performance pathways in the areas of Learning Disability, Physical Disability and Sensory Impairment and to develop an accessible Coach Education Strand which would improve the standard of coaching available to the disabled player.

Assistance was required in order to achieve these goals and in 2005 as part of the Youth Strategy, former Northern Ireland international, Mal Donaghy joined the Disability Football Department. His contribution has been immense.

*The NI Cerebral Palsy Squad meet Mary Peters before their match against Scotland at the Home Nations Cerebral Palsy Championships at University of Ulster.*

With support from an active Disability Football Steering Group, including members from RNIB, Special Olympics Ulster, Disability Sports NI, Sports Council, Special Education, Ulster Deaf Sports Council and the IFA, all of these objectives were achieved.

Some of the highlights in this period would be the formation of a Northern Ireland Cerebral Palsy Squad, the formation of Belfast Deaf United and their inclusion in the Down Area Winter League, a province-wide Visual Impairment Program and the International Learning Disability Squad finishing in 6th place in the 2006 World Cup ahead of countries such as England, France and Australia.

The Disability Department is embarking on a new five-year Development Strategy that maintains the previous objectives but also has a real emphasis on local provision of opportunities. The IFA is currently working in 32 of the 40 Special Schools in Northern Ireland and has helped form and develop over 40 Disability Football Clubs. There is also a clear performance pathway from participation, through competition to representation in the areas of Learning Disability, Cerebral Palsy, Deaf and Visually Impaired, but there are still limited opportunities for club involvement at local level and much work needs to be done. It is a challenge the Disability Department is determined to meet.

The IFA's aim is to ensure that all disabled people have the opportunity to take part in football activities and are able to fulfil their potential in the area of their choice. This admirable and hopefully attainable aim is very much part of the Association's 'Football For All' ethos.

*Michel Platini presents David Healy with an award for his goal-scoring achievement.*

# The Euro 2008 Campaign

The summer of 2008 could well have seen the biggest exodus of Northern Ireland supporters since the glory days of Espana '82. At the halfway stage it looked like Northern Ireland had a splendid chance of making the finals. Then the applecart was overturned.

The international manager Lawrie Sanchez decided to do a runner to the Premiership for what proved to be a miserable and short sojourn at Fulham. He deserted the team and the supporters he professed to be so dedicated to, and severely diminished any hopes they had of qualifying. Undoubtedly in his time Sanchez had

got some wonderful results in marquee games, notably against England and Spain. But his away record was poor and perhaps his 'barrow boy' instincts told him to quit while he was ahead.

Lawrie's decision left his successor Nigel Worthington with an impossible task. He had to get to know the players, gain their confidence and try to lift them again after the shock departure of the previous manager. He was also faced with four games away and just two at home. In the end the task proved to be a bridge too far.

*Kids with painted faces.*

But the players gave qualification a decent go, improved Northern Ireland's seeding for the World Cup qualifiers and helped to make a little bit of history. That came when David Healy broke Davor Suker's record of 12 goals scored during Croatia's qualifying campaign for Euro 1996. He finished the campaign with an amazing 13 goals. It was a wonderfully consistent goal-scoring spree which lit up Northern Ireland's campaign.

"The hat trick against Spain was the highlight," admitted Healy as he reflected on his achievement. "It was a hugely entertaining campaign for the players and fans alike."

Undoubtedly this was the case. The fans revelled in Healy's goals and the fact that the team were once more getting into a position to challenge for qualification. The

Green and White Army were absolutely delighted when their pin-up boy was formally recognized by UEFA for his incredible scoring run during the qualifying campaign. French legend turned legislator – and the current President of UEFA – Michel Platini travelled to Belfast to present 'wee Davy' with official recognition of his goal glut.

"His 13 goals is a new record and deserves to be recognized," ventured the great man. "I am sure it will last for some time, and I presented this special award to celebrate his fantastic achievement."

Healy's remarkable feat was sealed when he cheekily chipped in the winner in a 2-1 victory over Denmark in monsoon-like conditions at Windsor Park on 17 November 2007. In truth the game should never have

*Gareth McAuley kicks up spray during the Denmark game.*

*Northern Ireland fans in Copenhagen.*

started, and at times the pitch seemed more suited for a performance of 'Singin' In The Rain' than an important international football match. The ball repeatedly got held up in puddles of water on the flanks, and even the simplest of passes were often accompanied by a torrent of spray as soon as the ball was kicked, as our picture of Gareth McAuley demonstrates.

The record-breaking goal that Healy scored in that Denmark game helped temper the disappointment of not qualifying for the finals. Away defeats in Iceland and Latvia put the final nails in the qualification coffin, but the 3-0 defeat in the opening game against the Icelanders at Windsor Park had also proved costly.

On the plus side that sensational 3-2 win over Spain in Belfast which saw Northern Ireland twice come from behind to win, provided one of the greatest Windsor Park nights ever. The home win over Sweden plus a hugely credible away draw also offered immense encouragement. However, in the end Northern Ireland lost out to the Swedes and the Spanish. In the years to come when the campaign to qualify for Euro 2008 is talked about, the highlight will undoubtedly be those 13 goals scored by Healy.

But in the back of everyone's mind there will always be a nagging doubt about what might have been, had Sanchez stayed. He could well have spent the summer of 2008 as the first Northern Ireland manager to lead out the team at a major tournament since the great Billy Bingham.

*Top: Laganside Northern Ireland Supporters' Club in Riga, Latvia.*

*Bottom: Northern Ireland Fans in Riga, Latvia.*

Top: The boys celebrate their victory over Spain

Bottom: Fans celebrate in Copenhagen

# Billy Bingham – The Guv'nor

*Billy during his playing days.*

*A Souvenir 1982 World Cup Patch.*

Any fan worth his salt will tell you that Billy Bingham is synonymous with the good times for the Northern Ireland team. At the start of the qualifying campaign for the 2010 World Cup in South Africa, Northern Ireland still held the record for the most appearances by any small country in the finals.

The boys in green have been there on three occasions. The first was Sweden 1958, also the last time all four of the British home countries qualified at the same time. The second appearance was 1982 in Spain, followed by Mexico four years later.

The common thread in all three tournaments was Billy Bingham. He played in all five games in Sweden in 1958 when he was a formidable right winger playing for Sunderland in the old English First Division. Then in the 1980s he masterminded his country to Spain and Mexico as manager. His 1982 side in Spain managed to emulate the achievement of the team he played in twenty-four years earlier by getting to the quarter finals, before losing to France. While this was a marvellous achievement, many feel his finest hour was managing to squeeze a second World Cup qualification out of an ageing squad for Mexico 1986.

Bingham's success was built on meticulous preparation. His research was intense and wide ranging. Not only did it cover the opposition's players – he also sought to find out everything he could about where his Northern Ireland team would be playing. He took the squad to Brighton ahead of the 1982 World Cup in Spain. The weeks spent there were not just about training and tactics. Bingham also used them to enhance the camaraderie that already existed within the squad.

"His man-management was brilliant," remembers former striker Billy Hamilton. "He worked us hard, but he always knew when to tone things down. Then he would cut us a bit of slack and allow us a night out, but it was back to work next morning."

That spell in Brighton coincided with a heatwave on the south coast of England. But Bingham welcomed it, reasoning that it gave his players a taste of what was to come in Spain.

"I knew there was good chance that it would turn out that way in Brighton in early June," remembers Northern Ireland's greatest ever manager. "But while that meant the players were experiencing the sort of heat they could expect in Spain they were also in familiar surroundings, eating the sort of food they get at home and so on."

It worked a treat and it was during that World Cup that one of the biggest shocks ever in the World Cup took place, when little Northern Ireland defeated the host nation Spain 1-0 in Valencia to qualify for the quarter finals. Gerry Armstrong scored the winning goal after 47 minutes. Northern Ireland then played out a famous victory, despite playing the last 28 minutes of the game with ten men after Mal Donaghy was sent off.

Espana '82 demonstrated Bingham's knack of taking bold decisions and getting his reward. At that tournament he introduced a teenager called Norman Whiteside to international football. He played in all the Northern Ireland games. He also became the youngest player ever to appear in the World Cup when he lined out against Yugoslavia in the Estadio La Romereda, Zaragoza at just 17 years and 41 days, eclipsing the record set by the great Pele in Sweden seven years before Whiteside was born.

'Big Norm' announced his arrival on the world's biggest football stage by scoring after just 6 minutes. Feats like this were later to move his one-time Manchester United manager Ron Atkinson to describe him as "the ultimate big occasion player".

After watching him in Brighton, Bingham had no hesitation in putting him in the team. Although he did admit he had certain reservations later, during the match with Spain.

"The Spaniards' tackling was a bit uncompromising, and at one point Norman was hacked down ruthlessly from behind," recalls Bingham. "He was a seventeen-year-old kid and I was lost in thought on the bench wondering if I should have exposed him to all this. Suddenly a *thud* brought me right back to earth. It was the Spanish player who had fouled young Whiteside and Norman had taken an opportunity to show him two could play at that game. I knew immediately that he would be fine."

Bingham admits unashamedly that he was determined to have every angle covered for those World Cups. Take Mexico 1986 for example:

"I learned after the draw that we would be playing our games 5000 feet above sea level, so I immediately set about finding a suitable place for our training camp," he remembers. "My first port of call was the local library, and after much searching I decided that Albuquerque seemed to fit the bill. So then I homed in on it and set about finding out every single thing I could about it.

"Eventually I headed over there and searched around for a suitable training camp. I found it, and that was where we prepared for Mexico. Being in the United States it had all the infrastructure to keep the players happy, in terms of diet and things to do in their down time. But the best part was that it was 7000 feet above sea level – which I didn't tell the players initially. So after we had acclimatised to playing there, coping with 5000 feet for the tournament was much less of a problem."

This demonstrates Bingham's thorough approach and also his burning desire to be a winner. His Northern Ireland teams were always well drilled and well organised.

"Billy was a total one-off," explains Martin O'Neill, his captain in Spain. "He knew what he wanted from us as a squad, and his results speak for themselves."

'Bouncing Billy', as he was known for his all-action style during his playing days, also recognised that the fans need to be catered for and respected. He made the players as accessible to them as possible, and the players were always happy to oblige. The supporters appreciated this and also respected Bingham for his achievements.

Derek McKinley was at both the World Cups when Bingham managed the side. As kit man he was in the dressing room before, during and after all the big games.

"I have heard a few team talks in my time, but nobody ever came close to Billy in that department," reveals Derek. "He was not only a great motivator and an inspiration but he knew everything about every player we were playing against. He would stand up and talk and everyone paid attention. He also did it – remember – with no props. No power-point presentations, no flip boards, videos, DVDs or anything. It was all in his head, and he was magnificent at getting his points across."

*Billy pictured as manager.*

In 2008 there were various events for the fiftieth anniversary of Northern Ireland qualifying for their first World Cup in Sweden in 1958. The great men of the past who had outlived team mates from those bygone days were all shown total respect, and were treated most reverently. None more so than William Laurence Bingham. Still instantly recognised wherever he goes in Northern Ireland, he relished reliving the glory days.

*Meeting a Danish fan in Copenhagen.*

# THE
# GREEN AND WHITE
# ARMY

*Colin Murray with Michael Boyd of the IFA and Jim Rainey (centre) who was crowned 'NI Community Champion' for his charity, anti-sectarian and volunteer work.*

# Recognition for the Fans

In 2006 the Northern Ireland fans were recognised as the best in Europe, when they won the prestigious Brussels International Supporters Award.

Jim Rainey collected the prize on behalf of the Amalgamation of Northern Ireland Supporters' Clubs prior to the Spain game at Windsor Park in September of that year. Northern Ireland legend Billy Hamilton, one of the heroes of the 1982 World Cup in Spain, presented the award. It was important recognition of the tireless work that the Amalgamation had done.

Much is made – and rightly so – of their work to combat sectarianism and change the vocal landscape at Northern Ireland games. However, there is also a strong commitment to charity work embedded in the Amalgamation's culture.

At the time the award was presented the Amalgamation had raised over £82,000 for a variety of local charities and also funded needy causes in places like Azerbaijan and Armenia. That work continues and has been boosted by the proceeds from sales of 'We're Not Brazil, We're Northern Ireland'.

The song came out on CD during the Euro 2008 qualifying campaign. It features some fans, with broadcasters Jackie Fullerton and George Jones doing lead vocals.

It was recorded at the Mallusk studios of Emerald Music under the supervision of chart-busting record producer George Doherty, the man behind Jive Bunny and Roly Daniels.

"I was pleased with the way the session turned out," admits George. "The fans involved were very enthusiastic, and very patient because recording can be a convoluted process. Jackie and George are used to that but the fans involved soon got into the way of things. The CD has been well received, but since Sanchez did a runner we have had lots of calls asking could we change the line '*Now Lawrie is our leader and we're coming after you*', and substitute '*Nigel*' instead."

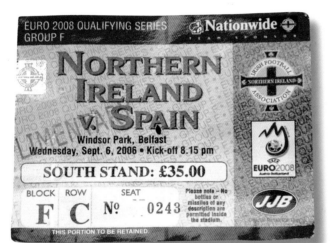

*A keepsake of hat-trick victory.*

The man behind 'We're Not Brazil, We're Northern Ireland' is Jim Rainey. He introduced the song to the fans as something which celebrated their identity and had no sectarian baggage. Ever the pragmatist, he printed out lyric sheets which were distributed before games at Windsor Park. That, of course, was in the early days. Now the song is embedded in everyone's psyche and has become as much a part of Northern Ireland games as queuing for the toilet and the 'bouncy'.

The Brussels International Supporters Award was important recognition for the hard work that the Amalgamation had done to make Windsor Park a family friendly venue.

Rainey, quietly delighted that the supporters' efforts had been rewarded, said on receiving the award: "We have used the spirit of football to extend the hand of friendship around the globe, while never missing an opportunity to help those less fortunate than ourselves."

The supporters' pro-active stance against sectarianism, plus their absolute determination to have as much fun as possible when watching their team, has given a new platform for the IFA to take things on to another level. The days when Windsor was perceived to be a place that was out of bounds to one section of the community are well and truly over. Only the most churlish would believe otherwise.

However what has not changed is the reluctance of some residents of Northern Ireland to come to support the team. The reason for this is very simple. These people do not subscribe to the notion that the State exists and prefer to go to Dublin and support the Republic. That is their choice and should be respected. But that respect also brings with it a responsibility on them to admit their reasons for doing so are not that they feel excluded, but they have no wish to be included. Those who suggest they could only contemplate attending future Northern Ireland games in the 'shared space' of a new national stadium are fooling nobody. They could not contemplate attending Northern Ireland games because their hearts and loyalties lie elsewhere. End of story.

So how did the Northern Ireland supporters come to receive this award? How did the people in Brussels come to be aware of their efforts?

"Michael Boyd heard that an organisation over in Brussels was looking for examples of cross-community activity, and he decided to enter the Amalgamation for the work that they did at Windsor in trying to eradicate sectarian singing at International games," explains Rainey. "He decided to enter us on that basis, and listed all the things that I did and what my role within the Amalgamation was. It was the second year of the award – the inaugural year it was won by a group in Italy – and it was presented the night we beat Spain 3-2. A memorable evening all round.

"After the match they said they were hugely impressed that the Northern Ireland fans gave total respect to the Spanish national anthem and their support for the team and that they had thoroughly deserved the award. The good thing about winning it in 2006 was that it was World Cup year and the runners up were the German fans, for their behaviour during the tournament when they made everyone so welcome, so the competition was pretty stiff."

The Green and White Army have become an asset to Northern Ireland in several ways. Not only are they 'the extra man' when the team play, with their loud, raucous and good-humoured support, but they portray the country in a positive light when they travel abroad.

They also work well with the IFA who have tried to make them feel part of everything that is happening. Undoubtedly there are areas where the two camps disagree. The prospect of a new national stadium at the Maze being one major and obvious example, and the control of distribution of tickets for home games a lesser one. Just like in any family there will always be disagreements, but in the end the common good prevails. Such is the relationship between the IFA and the Amalgamation.

Once the stadium situation is resolved there will be increased opportunities for both to develop their roles in an enhanced environment. One thing the pair have in common is a commitment not to rest on their laurels. Both Geoff Wilson and Jim Rainey see their successes to date as very much a work in progress. Given that mixture of realism and the determination to finish the job, building on their success to date, it would seem that the Green and White Army will continue their march fervently, hoping that qualification for a major tournament will be at the end of the road.

# The Lows...

If winning the prestigious Brussels International Supporters' Award in 2006 was the pinnacle for the Green and White Army the low point was undoubtedly Neil Lennon's exit from the international arena.

Neil Lennon

Ahead of a friendly international against Cyprus in August 2002, in which he was due to captain the side, Lennon was the subject of a death threat. It was phoned to the BBC in Belfast and purported to come from the Loyalist Volunteer Force. Although the recognized code word was not given by the caller, the police took it seriously.

They advised Lennon to "look carefully at his personal security" even though the LVF had declared the threat to be a hoax and nothing to do with their terrorist organisation. Lennon decided to call it quits, and never played for Northern Ireland again.

"I can't put my family through this every time," said the Celtic midfielder back then. "It's a real pity that it all had to end like this."

But it did. Lennon's exit was the final act in a tawdry chapter that shamed Northern Ireland international football and its supporters. The player's problems began when he moved from Leicester City to Celtic. When he appeared for Northern Ireland against Norway at Windsor Park in February 2001 he was booed by a section of the crowd, every time he touched the ball.

"There was a group of fans, sixty to a hundred maybe, who were sitting at the back of the stand and were Rangers supporters," remembers one Northern Ireland regular. "There were not many of them, but it was not a good night for the home side who went on to lose 4-0 and the crowd was quiet. That meant that the anti-Lennon brigade sounded a lot noisier."

The booing of a player for the home side bewildered the visitors, and was an acute embarrassment for the IFA and the Northern Ireland fans. Lennon was substituted at half time. The actions of the so-called supporters who booed him were roundly condemned, but it left a bad taste.

Lennon played the following month in a World Cup qualifier against the Czech Republic, and was loudly cheered every time he touched the ball. He also featured in home and away defeats by Bulgaria, and then played what was to prove to be his last game in a green shirt in a friendly with Poland.

Next up was that game against Cyprus. It should have been his proudest moment, as he was scheduled to skipper the Northern Ireland team. Then came that death threat which killed off any prospect of the Lurgan-born carrot top ever playing for Northern Ireland again. It was a classic case of a few bigots ruining things for everyone. But the Amalgamation knew it had to be pro-active in bringing on back the good times.

The journey to that particular Promised Land required patience, ingenuity and tenacity. It is a credit to the Amalgamation and indeed the IFA that they got there. But the reality is that the journey should never have been necessary in the first place.

# ...On the Up

It was against a pretty bleak background that Michael Boyd took the job as Head of Community Relations at the IFA in February 2000. At that stage people were queuing up to tell him it was probably the worst job in the world, and certainly the worst one in football. Northern Ireland fans had been labelled as sectarian ostriches, with neither the interest nor desire to change.

"Everybody told me that I would never get the fans to change. They were seen as a bunch of bigots," remembers Michael. "They said my job was mission impossible. But I never saw it like that, nor did I go into it with a negative approach.

"The first fax I got on taking up the post was from the Shankill Northern Ireland Supporters' Club. It said they would support community relations initiatives at the IFA. So I invited the Amalgamation of NI Supporters' Clubs into a meeting at the IFA. They were amazed to be invited into the building, and each club sent two delegates.

"At that stage there were just ten clubs and now it is over one hundred. It was a difficult meeting because the fans had many issues with the IFA, from car parking to toilet facilities, the stadium and so on. But the meeting was specifically about our 'Football For All' campaign. I had to keep returning to that, and the need to create an atmosphere that would encourage families to come back. Since that day there has always been an open and transparent line of communication between the fans and the IFA, and I am the conduit for that.

"We invited two fans to be representatives on our 'Football For All' community relations advisory panel. That got them involved at a strategic level and it banished the fear of any hidden agendas or whatever. We wanted to create a fun, safe and inclusive football environment and the Amalgamation

*Michael Boyd wins an award for services to local football from Stewart McAfee on behalf of the Amalgamation of Supporters' Clubs.*

and the Green and White Army bought into that, and have been at the heart of those changes."

The trust that Michael has built up with the fans has led to the carnival atmosphere, which has become an integral part of Northern Ireland's home games. The sectarian songs have been eradicated. The 'Billy Boys' replaced by 'We're Not Brazil, We're Northern Ireland', 'Sweet Caroline' and other anthems, often to a distinctive samba beat.

It is often said that to achieve success you sometimes need to take risks. Leap forward in good faith. Michael did just that shortly after taking his job at the IFA, by pleading with his bosses to lift their ban on drums inside Windsor Park and allow in one guy with his Lambeg drum.

The drummer in question came from the City of Armagh NI Supporters' club and in a bizarre twist was called David Trimble! The IFA allowed him to bring his drum but on one

*Playing a samba beat.*

condition – Michael had to stand beside him to ensure that it was not used for sectarian purposes. Michael takes up the story:

"He used the drum for songs free of sectarianism, but when small pockets of fans in the Kop tried to start some sectarian chants or songs he drowned them out with a samba beat. This sent out a powerful message that NI fans were no longer prepared to tolerate sectarianism. So taking that calculated risk with the drummer had paid off.

"It was the start of a relationship built on trust between the IFA and the fans, and it planted the seeds for them to be at the heart of the 'Football For All' campaign. A small but significant example of fan power pro-actively eradicating sectarianism from the terraces."

*The Green and White Army in full voice.*

# Jim Rainey

Jim Rainey has worked tirelessly to give the image of the Northern Ireland supporters a makeover in recent years. If Michael Boyd's job in community relations at the IFA was being dubbed 'the worst job in football', Jim's quest was more about realising a dream. An impossible dream suggested many, and on the face of it they were right. But Rainey had the determination to see it through and realised that the best strategy was one step at a time.

He knew that the key to progress was to get the supporters more organised and under one umbrella. So he was at the forefront of getting the Amalgamation of Northern Ireland Supporters' Clubs to become a more united, a more far reaching and above all a more organised body. The Amalgamation has been to the forefront in improving the atmosphere at Windsor Park over the past few years, but how did the organisation initially come about?

"Back in the 1980s there were only about three or four Northern Ireland supporters' clubs", says Jim Rainey, "and these were formed around the time of the 1982 and 1986 World Cups, when the team was enjoying tremendous success. The only ones that kept going though were clubs like 1st Shankill and the South Belfast, who had their own licensed premises. Then in 1999 a few more clubs emerged such as Laganside and Harbour Bar and it was suggested we should get a bit more organised.

"At that stage no one was affiliated with the IFA. So initially we came together and had a meeting at Windsor Park. We then approached the IFA to see if they would officially recognize us. They readily agreed to this so we formed the Amalgamation with a total of eleven clubs, and now that has grown to over eighty."

The Amalgamation is not just confined to Belfast though, as Jim explains:

"In Northern Ireland, we have clubs stretching from Londonderry, Castlederg, Armagh, Enniskillen and Craigavon, in fact right around the whole Province. People have the impression that the Amalgamation is a Belfast-

45

*Jim Rainey.*

"The Spirit of '82 and the North Coast clubs would both boast over 100 members, but the others, because of accommodation, travel and tickets try to keep it to around 25-30 which is a more manageable figure. So all in all I would imagine there are around 3000 individual members attached to clubs in the Amalgamation."

Following the 'Neil Lennon Affair' in 2002, Northern Ireland fans were, unfairly, due to the action of a small and vociferous group of morons, classed as sectarian and bigots. So how has the Amalgamation managed to radically change the atmosphere at Windsor to what it is today?

"We had this idea to create singing sections in two of the stands. We agreed with the IFA to have 800 fans from the Amalgamation sit together in the West Stand and 200 in the North Stand. Whenever there was any sectarian singing I would get the megaphone out and start up songs like 'We're Not Brazil, We're Northern Ireland' or 'Stand Up for the Ulstermen' so as to drown out any unsavoury chants. Nowadays though there is nothing to drown out!

"I have always said the IFA could not have achieved this on their own. They could have had a Community Relations department at Windsor Avenue, but unless the fans had bought into it the change would never have happened. Likewise the fans needed the IFA, because they needed the financial backing they gave for such initiatives as the 'Sea of Green' campaign."

The Amalgamation is also heavily into fund raising and over the past nine years the organisation has raised nearly £100,000 for charities in far off places such as Azerbaijan and Armenia.

"Prior to going to Armenia in 2002 we decided to donate clothes and colouring pens and toys to an orphanage in Yerevan that we became aware of. We contacted the British Consul to organise everything and eventually had about 50 mail bags of items flown over on the IFA charter. We have of course donated money to various other causes over the years, but

based organisation, but out of the eighty-odd clubs there are only about ten in and around the Belfast area. Every second meeting will be held outside of the capital, so everyone has the opportunity to attend them.

"We also have some further afield; we have the North and South of England clubs and the Scottish supporters clubs. Then there is one in the Far East, in America and Australia, and I also run a Worldwide Supporters' Club via the internet, and that has over one hundred members.

*Windsor Park becomes family friendly.*

that side of being a Northern Ireland fan never gets reported, because good news stories never sell papers, do they?"

So what does Jim feel the future holds for the Northern Ireland team? And does he feel that the bad old days of bigotry at Windsor Park are now a thing of the past?

"I don't feel we will ever drift back into the days of 1970s and 1980s, when there was a fair amount of sectarian chanting. But you have to be aware that Northern Ireland is Northern Ireland and things like this could creep in again if we don't continue with our work. But you have to be careful you don't go too far, because some people are saying that we are the 'happy-clappy PC mob' and they don't want to be a part of that.

"For example, if a fan goes to a Northern Ireland game with his Irish League shirt on, he should not be scoffed at by other supporters because they feel he should be wearing green and white, the colours of his country. We don't want to alienate Irish League fans, so if they want to go and support their country in a Linfield or Glentoran top that is their prerogative."

In 2006 the Northern Ireland fans were recognised as the best in Europe when they won the prestigious Brussels International Supporters' Award, with Jim collecting the prize on behalf of the Amalgamation prior to the September game against the Spanish at Windsor Park.

# *Jonny Blair*

Jonny Blair, who originally hails from Bangor, is the colourful chairman of the South of England Northern Ireland Supporters' Club which was formed in late 2005. With a membership of 43 the club holds regular meetings right across the South of England. So how did the SOE Northern Ireland Supporters' Club originate, and what were the reasons behind setting up such a club?

*Jonny Blair*

"I moved over to live in Bournemouth in 2003 as I was going to University, and had been flying back 'home' for every Northern Ireland match in Belfast, so the enthusiasm was there. I began to wonder if there were other people around my area doing the same thing, and whether it was possible to start a club up like the ones in London, the North of England and in Scotland.

"I randomly happened to go to the Poland away game in March 2005, when I first encountered founder member Tim Beattie in a bar in Berlin. (We were both going to Poland via Berlin!) It transpired that Tim was living on the South Coast as well, in Southampton. The day after we met we both got a train from Berlin to Warsaw, and on that train we met another founder member of the club, Owen Millar, who was at that time living in Bristol.

"I then went to the England game at Windsor in September 2005 and there was a huge buzz around the place, especially after the outcome of the match, so Tim and I decided that the time was now right to set up the South of England Supporters' Club. I already knew a few other people from Northern Ireland who lived in the area and got them on board as well, then to attract more members we put a post on the 'Our Wee Country' website. That was late in 2005.

*South England NISC meet Sammy Clingan*

"Members are based from Plymouth to Dartford in Kent so it is quite a spread. However our meetings are normally held in a smaller geographical area, around Brighton, Weymouth and Southampton, though we do try and visit as many different locations around the South that we can.

"We are always received with open arms wherever we go; we are welcomed into bars, clubs, football stadiums, and we like to add a bit of colour (usually green) and madness to anywhere we go. We dress up in green wigs and take along green crocodiles, and basically just have a good day out. Though I also like to think of ourselves as ambassadors for our wee country, telling English people how great a place Northern Ireland is, and how great the people are."

Like many other Northern Ireland Supporters' Clubs, the SOE branch also raises and donates money to charities.

"We are only a small supporters' club but every time we have an event, which is usually every couple of months, we all dip our hands in our pocket to raise some money for a charity which is local to where we are having our meeting. It might only be £50 or £100 but the charities appreciate it. So far we have given money to the 'Mountbatten Hospice' on the Isle of Wight, the Cherries Nursing Home in Weymouth among others, and we even donated some money to the George Best Foundation around the time of his death. However I'm hoping that over the next few years we can do something major on the charity front. Although for the start of the 2008-09 season we are donating a football kit to a youth team somewhere along the South Coast."

Jonny has been attending Northern Ireland games since 1990, and feels the support 'Our Wee Country' receives today is a lot more passionate and less sectarian than when he went to his first international against Yugoslavia at Windsor Park.

"The support is a lot more vociferous than it was in that first game. There is a lot more singing and enthusiasm, and a lot more tolerance among the fans these days for who and what you are. It really shouldn't matter what part of Northern Ireland you are from. If you are there to support the team you are there to support the team. We've had all the history of the Troubles and all the politics of 'Our Wee Country', and that has shaped football here in many ways.

"If you look back at some of the videos of the 1980s and early 1990s you will see a lot of 'boys' dressed in red, white and blue wearing Rangers and Linfield tops and scarves. That's not the image I believe Northern Ireland fans want, because it will alienate certain sections of the population who might otherwise come along and support the side.

"I think people now go to Northern Ireland games dressed in green and white and watching eleven players dressed in green shirts, and religion is out the window. There is no need to think about religion or sing any songs to do with Catholic or Protestant heritage because we have our own heritage, which is a Northern Irish heritage. The support today is phenomenal and it is down largely to making everyone feel welcome. Whether they are a five-year-old or an eighty-year-old, everybody really enjoys going to Windsor Park now.

"I think the IFA and especially Michael Boyd should take a lot of credit for this. Michael introduced a 'Football for All' initiative when he came into the job, at a time when Northern Ireland fans were being vilified because of the Neil Lennon incident. It is a really good time to be from Northern Ireland, not just because the football team are doing so well, but politically we are the strongest we have been for many years."

On the pitch Jonny feels the turnaround in Northern Ireland's fortunes occurred not when Lawrie Sanchez was appointed, but when Lawrie McMenemy left the managerial post after an ill-fated, eighteen-month stay in October 1999.

"Personally I feel our good run began and our support increased the day that McMenemy left the job. When Sammy McIlroy took over the reigns himself the team showed a lot more fight and passion – something that was totally lacking during the McMenemy era. The fans appreciated this and started turning up in greater numbers.

"The scoring drought kind of helped us a bit as well, as the sort of humour we have in Northern Ireland meant that the fans found it funny that we hadn't scored in 13 games. It seemed the longer the run went on the more the support pulled together and backed the team even more.

"Even though McIlroy was a Belfast boy with a bit of grit and determination, it was only when Sanchez came in that we managed to get it right on the pitch. Ever since Healy scored that goal in the 4-1 defeat by Norway in Sanchez's opening game – to end our scoreless run – we have been on a continuous high.

"There have been many highlights since that Norway game, but for me the best was when we beat Sweden 2-1 at Windsor Park, to go top of our European Qualifying Group. The reason I have chosen this game over the victories against England and Spain is because I never thought that we would ever be top of a group that contained Spain, Sweden and Denmark. Yet there we were halfway through the campaign, ahead of them all.

"Naturally the bubble will burst one day and the team will go back to probably struggling once again, but I believe the support will continue for the side. Of course people who have jumped on the bandwagon to follow Northern Ireland because they have been doing well recently will stop coming, but the real diehard fans, of whom I think I am one, will still be there cheering and singing the team on."

# "There's Always One" – Shaun Schofield

During his time in following Northern Ireland Shaun Schofield has on occasions been more than just a supporter.

"When I went with the team to Albania in 1993 I ended up staying in the team hotel and cooking for the players. It all came about when the IFA General Secretary David Bowen, requested that any supporters with catering experience report to Chef Tom Nesbitt – who needed assistance in the kitchen as the Albanian authorities had decided not to offer help in the form of catering staff.

"Having worked in kitchens during college vacations, I offered my services as requested, and ended up cooking bread in a stone oven, and attempting to boil potatoes on a gas hob with the heat strength of a match. Steak and roast chicken, two veg and, yes, boiled potatoes and hot bread did eventually appear 110 times, quite how though I am still not sure."

Shaun has been following Northern Ireland since 1993 and has not missed a single international home or away since June 1995. But that achievement is made all the more remarkable by the fact that Shaun is an Englishman with no connections to the Province. He has become a well-known figure at Windsor Park and on Northern Ireland away trips. In 2005 he wrote a book about his experiences in following his adopted country. He donated all the profits of *There's Always One – Ten Years of Watching Northern Ireland* to charity.

*Shaun Schofield presents Lawrie Sanchez with a copy of 'There's Always One'.*

"I started to travel and watch England during the 1990 World Cup in Italy and didn't miss a game for about three years; I went all round the world watching them in places like Turkey, Holland and America. In the end it just got to the stage where there was too much violence, and I decided that I had had enough. My first Northern Ireland game was on 17 February 1993 when they played Albania in Tirana, and I've still got my ticket of that match. Not to mention my chef's hat!

"I have found there is a massive difference between watching England and Northern Ireland: for a start there is a lot more camaraderie among the Irish fans. At Northern Ireland games people want speak to you and that has always been the case, whether it is with the ten supporters who travelled to the Ukraine in 1997 or the 4000 fans who went to Spain in 2006."

So during the past 15 years of supporting 'our wee country', how have things changed?

"Well for a start I think the supporters clubs' are a lot more organised. When I first started to going to Northern Ireland away games you might see some of the Shankill Road guys, or some from Dungannon but it was very hit or miss. These days it is much more organised and has grown ten-fold with the IFA and the Amalgamation of Supporters' clubs both running away trips.

"The IFA have also got their act together with regards merchandising. I remember that before I went on that Albania trip in 1993 I had to order the replica top from a specialised sports shop in Carnaby Street in London, and had to wait up to two weeks to get it! I have to admit when I first started coming to Belfast I didn't wear a Northern Ireland shirt in the street as I was quite worried that if someone saw it they might construe it in the wrong manner. Now though it's brilliant. Everyone is wearing Northern Ireland tops."

So how did it come about that he decided to write a book about following Northern Ireland?

"It was as simple as someone passing a comment at the airport once, that I had been to all these Northern Ireland games, so why didn't I write a book about my experiences? So I did!! It became something of a labour of love, and I got a lot of friends and family involved in the project. In all I printed 1040 copies and sold 1025 and in total I gave away around £9,500 to various charities.

"I have to say the IFA were excellent in their support. I initially discussed my business plan with them and they allowed me to use the IFA crest on the book, which gave the book a good mark of authenticity. I got Lawrie [Sanchez] to do the Foreword, and the IFA sold the book in their shop at Windsor Avenue. They waived any handling charges and in total sold 325 books. They were brilliant. I know they have their faults but on this occasion I can't praise them enough."

The atmosphere at Windsor Park these days is now renowned throughout Europe, but Shaun remembers too well what it was like when he first started to watch Northern Ireland in the early nineties.

"When I first went to Windsor Park, there were a lot of sectarian songs sung and a lot of banners up one of which I always remember said 'no ceasefire at Windsor Park', which was interesting as just one week before the game the IRA had announced a ceasefire. You go to Windsor now though, and there is no negative support, national anthems are taken on board in perfect silence, and it is a great place to be.

"In my mind though it's just a pity that Northern Ireland don't have a better stadium to play in. Personally I would put £25 million into getting Windsor Park sorted out. As for whether the new stadium should be built at the Maze, I'm ambivalent as to where they play. Windsor is over 100 years old and it looks it – sort it out or build anew!"

There have been many ups and downs during his fifteen-year dedication to the international side and one of the best occasions had to be September 2005 when Northern Ireland humbled the mighty England.

"Without question the 1-0 victory over England has been the ultimate highlight – because it was great

*Aaron Hughes greets fellow captain David Beckham before the historic victory over England.*

just to get one over them for a change – and I was still recovering from the result four days later. The recent wins over Spain and Denmark were also great experiences, as they were matches that really mattered and put us in a good position to qualify for Euro 2008. Those moments far outweigh times like the scoring drought and the dying embers of the Lawrie McMenemy era."

# 'Our Wee Country' Website

N Ireland fan site -
www.ourweecountry.co.uk

Marty Lowry is a Senior NCO in the Air Force and has been attending Northern Ireland games both home and away since the late 1970s. Having previously produced the fanzine *Our Wee Country*, Marty decided to prepare for the 21st century by going on the worldwide web in 1999. He runs the 'Our Wee Country' internet forum, which allows Northern Ireland supporters both at home and abroad the chance to communicate with each other on a wide range of subjects.

"With the help of Martin Harris, who currently helps run the Official IFA and Irish League websites, I set up the 'Our Wee Country' site. Since its inception it has become a focal point for Northern Ireland fans as regards everything relating to the international team. We have at present 7000 members, though I would say we have around 1000 who post regularly on the

site. However, a lot of people are just happy to look in on us and read what's going on."

Apart from helping fans with travel tips Marty has also in the past been instrumental in arranging charity football matches between Northern Ireland supporters and fans from other countries.

"The first of these games was played back in 1997 when we took on Germany at Dundela Football Club's ground Wilgar Park, and I think we lost 7-4. It was a tremendous day and we made many friends among our German counterparts.

"Despite organising that game to raise money to buy sports equipment for integrated schools in both Belfast and Newcastle, no help was forthcoming from the IFA. There was little response either from the numerous companies we wrote to in an attempt to gain sponsorship for the game. We did manage to get the-then Northern Ireland manager Bryan Hamilton to donate an autographed ball as a raffle prize though!

"Members of 'Our Wee Country' have also been responsible in the past for donating football shirts to charities in Azerbaijan and the website is currently sponsors of the Northern Ireland Cerebral Palsy football team."

Marty's first 'live' Northern Ireland was when his Dad brought him to the famous 1975 match with Yugoslavia at Windsor Park at the age of six.

"Not surprisingly I don't remember much about it, however the first game I can clearly recall being at was in 1977 against Holland, and I started to go to Windsor on a regular basis from about 1981-88, when I moved from Northern Ireland to England.

"My first ever away trip was in 1995 when I went to Riga in Latvia. The only other people I remember being there were the boys from the Shankill Road NISC and Shaun Schofield. Of course these days you can get anything from 2000 to 3000 fans travelling with the team, but it hasn't always been like that. I remember in Azerbaijan in 2004 there were only about eighty of us, while there was only around one hundred fans who travelled to Switzerland a few years ago. Larger numbers did make it to places like Germany and Portugal but only because these countries were easily accessible for people.

"Away trips are really like social occasions. I could go a year without seeing somebody, but meet them on a Northern Ireland away trip and you would be sitting chatting away to them as if you had only met them yesterday. The people come from all areas of the Province as well. I have made friends with guys from Fermanagh, Tyrone and Ballymena among others, and all because we had the same love of following our national team abroad.

"Today though we are getting thousands of fans travelling to support the team, and to be honest I don't think it is as enjoyable, as sometimes you obviously get your percentage of idiots going as well, intent on only causing trouble. Thankfully they are very much in the minority though, and most Northern Ireland supporters go out to have a good time."

Marty has no doubt about his best moment supporting 'our wee country'.

"The England game was a tremendous experience. My only regret was that because I now live in England I wasn't able to walk into work the next morning and see the look on the faces of my work colleagues! The Spain game and Healy's hat trick both run a very close second, but the England win will, I think, not be surpassed for a generation.

"Obviously there have been lots of low points following Northern Ireland. Not qualifying for Euro 2008 must be one of the lowest though. Those two defeats to Latvia and Iceland in the space of four days just ruined all the hard work we had put in previously. Funnily enough the non-scoring run we had wasn't that depressing. Towards the end we were getting ridiculed and laughed at by the mainstream press, but the fans' reaction was that it didn't matter. The crowds at Windsor actually went up!"

With regards the long-running stadium debate Marty has strong views, that Northern Ireland's new home should be built in Belfast and not on the outskirts of the city at somewhere like the Maze.

"Basically the stadium situation has to be sorted out, and sorted out quickly. We are desperately in need of a bigger ground with say a 20,000 to 25,000 capacity, I don't believe it should be any larger than that because when the bubble burst, as it naturally will, crowds will drop and you could end up playing in a half-empty stadium. We need a ground similar in design to that of Reading or Hull, but it has to be in Belfast. Plus the stadium I believe should be just for football, not GAA or Rugby, as they are already well catered for."

*David Healy and Keith Gillespie celebrate victory over Spain.*

# Green and White Spotlights

# JAKE BURNS (STIFF LITTLE FINGERS)

Second from right: Jake Burns (in NI top).

Rock star Jake Burns has been a lifelong Northern Ireland fan. At the time of the 1982 World Cup he and the other members of Stiff Little Fingers were living in London and were in the process of recording an album.

"Henry Cluney and myself used to slip away from the recording sessions to watch the Northern Ireland games which brassed off the others at the studio," remembers Jake. "Then on the day they were due to play the hosts Spain, I developed a very heavy cold. It was one of those ones which floors you. I phoned in to say I couldn't make the session. Of course nobody at the studio believed me. They all thought I had skived off to watch the Northern Ireland game at home.

"So there I am lying in bed watching the match on television, feeling very sorry for myself. I caught a glimpse of myself in the mirror, and even though I felt awful I had to laugh. I was lying there wearing my Northern Ireland scarf. It looked ridiculous. The game was going on and I felt crap and probably looked it as well.

"Then Gerry Armstrong scores and I leap up in the bed, cheering and shouting like mad. But there is still quite a while to go. I'm lying there willing Northern Ireland, now down to ten men, to hold out. Suddenly it's over.

"We've won. I want to celebrate. But I'm stuck there on my own. So I make the supreme effort, drag myself out of bed and head off down to the pub still wearing my Northern Ireland scarf. I wander in and the others from the studio, where recording of the 'Now Then' album has been suspended, are all sitting there having a few pints. 'Oh look, effin' Lazarus has come to join us,' they say. Recording resumed the next day and I still felt awful but everyone insisted it was a hangover so it was back to work.

"I loved that '82 team and the way they confounded everybody. In England the word was that Northern Ireland would be the first of the UK teams to come home, but we stayed longest. I used to love watching Martin O'Neill, a real Rolls-Royce of a player. The thing that struck me about him was that he always seemed to have all the time in the world. Despite being a Newcastle fan I even managed to put aside my anti-United feelings when big Norman Whiteside was playing. Great days.

"But there have been a few of those recently too, especially that 1-0 win over England. The day it happened we had visitors from England staying at my home in Chicago. We had been showing them the sights, and unusually I couldn't find a pub where the game was on. We had settled for a few pints and mates who were at the match or watching it on TV in England kept texting me.

"It was all along the lines of 'they still haven't scored', 'it's still 0-0' and so on. Then I get one which says that David Healy had scored and I jump out of my seat punching the air. My English friends, who have no interest in football plus the Americans in this downtown Chicago bar, all think I have lost my reason. Then of course there is that awful wait to see if Northern Ireland can hold out.

"When the text comes through that the game is over and that Healy's goal has won it I'm off again. Dancing around the bar giving my English friends the fingers shouting: 'We beat you, we beat you!' They look at me and say: 'We couldn't care less about football. Why are you getting at us?'

"'Because you're the only English people here!' I scream. "Crazy or what?"

## GEORGE JONES (BROADCASTER AND MUSICIAN)

"Whenever I was asked to take over the pre- and post-match broadcasting duties at Northern Ireland's home games at Windsor Park, I think the IFA just wanted someone to drown out the sectarian singing.

"I asked for a free hand to play music the fans could sing along to, and was given *carte blanche*. So I began to play things I felt the fans would like. We also passed request slips around for birthday requests and so on, and also to get a handle on what the fans wanted. Things like 'We Are The Champions', 'Is This The Way To Amarillo' and 'Sweet Caroline' proved to be big favourites. After a slow start and support and help from the Amalgamation of NI Supporters Clubs things began to turn around.

"Roy Kitson is there to help me. He knows a lot about football and introduces the foreign teams while I do Northern Ireland. David Hull booked in circus acts and things for the kids in the pre-match, and there were youngsters playing five-a-sides on the pitch at half time.

"The idea was to put the emphasis back on families again. The most important thing was to keep pumping out the music and set the atmosphere so that it would not drift into any songs of a sectarian nature. We had to get away from all that. I was also trying to create a carnival atmosphere, bringing the fans along with me and then impressing on them the need to show the world that Northern Ireland was a fun place.

"Paramount in all this was that we needed to show respect for all national anthems. I used to pre-announce them by saying 'Come on Northern Ireland! The eyes of the world are upon us. Let us give the best of attention and respect for the national anthems. It worked. It was gradual, mind you. For the first few games there were still a few people not buying into it. But the other fans around them weren't having that. They felt the reputation of their country was at stake and it soon stopped. Now at Windsor Park there is total silence during the playing of the anthems of visiting teams.

"It's now a family friendly place, and I have portrayed that fact on my daily radio show on U105. The crowds have grown. The home games sell out and we now have a team to be proud of . But the bottom line is that what has happened is the magic of what the fans have made themselves. It is a credit to them that things have turned around so radically. People like me and others have helped, but for it to happen at all the fans had to want it to. They have shown to the world that they did."

*George Jones*

# PAUL CHARLES (MURDER MYSTERY NOVELIST AND MUSIC MOGUL)

Paul Charles

"When I first moved across to London in 1967 it wasn't so much that there wasn't a national (Northern Irish) pride, but more that I hadn't even realised I'd an accent. People started to give me a second glance along their noses though when they heard my foreign Magherafelt tones. They'd recite my vocal peculiarities back at me as they checked my jacket for hardware.

"Then along came George Best, Alex Higgins, Van Morrison, James Galway and The Undertones, and you couldn't help but notice the old head growing taller, if not bigger.

"And then on 23 May 1972 didn't the amazing Northern Ireland football team only go and thrash the very recent (but not *most* recent) World Champions, England 1-0 at Wembley. The only goal scored by Terry Neill. I always found it funny, not to mention accurate, that when Northern Ireland beat England 1-0, it's a 'thrashing', but when England get lucky against Northern Ireland (4-0) it's was always a match that 'could have gone either way'.

"But that was pretty much it for a few decades, until along came the genius David Healy and the gang, who thrashed England another resounding 1-0 on 7 September 2005. Beckham, Rooney and Co. looked in genuine shock as they meekly scurried off Windsor Park. The reality they'd failed to grasp was that the Northern Ireland players are most certainly amongst the best in the world, but it took Lawrie Sanchez to instil this belief in the players themselves.

"Perhaps if Sanchez had not jumped ship mid-contract, with the combination of him and those players, we'd most certainly have qualified for the current Euro 2008 Championship. And you know what? I would have quite fancied the Northern Irish team to give the Spanish another 3-2 thrashing in the final!

"Mind you, there's always the World Cup; we don't want the big boys from the wee North peaking too soon, now do we?"

# GERRY ARMSTRONG (SKY PUNDIT/NORTHERN IRELAND LEGEND)

"My memories of the Northern Ireland fans from my playing days are all good," recalls Gerry Armstrong. "But then they are a very discerning group of supporters and they took to me for two reasons, I think. Firstly, I always gave 100 per cent and secondly I scored two goals on my debut, a 3-0 win over Belgium. The first one was a right foot shot which roared into the top corner. I knocked in the second one with my left foot after rounding the keeper.

"I played in a great era. Between 1980-86 we were undefeated at Windsor Park. It was a fortress. Obviously one of the biggest nights for me was scoring the goal when we defeated Israel to qualify for 'Espana '82'. There were forty thousand people crammed into Windsor Park that night, and once we had won the game and made the finals it was partytime.

"Then when we got to Spain the fans really came into their own. They sang their hearts out wherever we played, and were welcomed anywhere they went because of their fun-loving attitude. Obviously those were wonderful times but the fans today are a bit special too. They travel in their thousands to support the Northern Ireland team and never cause any bother.

"Although everyone talks about the wins over England, Spain and Sweden in recent times for me the fans really came into their own in September 2004 at Cardiff. There must have been ten thousand of them who made the journey to Wales and they took over the centre of Cardiff to the extent that they seemed to outnumber the home fans. Inside the Millennium Stadium that carried on – the noise level was incredible and they even managed to out-sing the Welsh fans. Now, given the tradition of singing in Wales that was no mean feat.

"I must admit that on that occasion when the game was over I felt a considerable sense of frustration. It finished 2-2 if you remember, but we were leading 2-0 at one point. But then

*Gerry in action against Spain in 1982.*

with Michael Hughes and then David Healy being sent off in controversial circumstances by the Italian referee Domenico Messina, the lads did well to hold on for almost three-quarters of the game.

"The fans have had their critics in recent times, especially around the Neil Lennon controversy, but full credit to the IFA and above all the fans themselves for the hard work they have done, to turn things around completely."

# COLIN MURRAY (RADIO 1 AND 5LIVE BROADCASTER AND THE IFA'S 'FOOTBALL FOR ALL' AMBASSADOR)

*From left: Colin Murray with Amalgamation of Official Northern Ireland Supporters' Clubs members – Ricky McIntyre, Phil Smyth and NI Community Champion Jim Rainey, the IFA's Michael Boyd, former international Bryan Hamilton and the Amalgamation's Gary McAllister.*

"In March 2008 I was invited by the Irish Football Association as 'Football For All' Ambassador to present the awards at their Community Champions event at the Grosvenor House. Looking back at the year that was, I asked for a list of all events and award winners.

"The emails came thick and fast... our Inaugural FFA Awards night; the FFA Conference; the IFA Anti-Racist month; the World Untied Consultation; the Unity Cup; the winning of the MAMA award in Dublin and so on and so on. And then I received the winners' names, all of them more than worthy of being singled out as key players in the change of landscape surrounding the supporting of our national football team.

"At the FFA Awards night, I was truly honoured to be entrusted with handing the awards over to such outstanding recipients. However, I would also wager a significant amount of crisp banknotes that none of them, in keeping with the overall humility and team ethos of the Northern Irish support, are very comfortable in the spotlight. None of them, I would predict, tell stories in bars on Saturday nights about just how special and important they are.

"So, instead, I'd like to metaphorically award every Northern Ireland fan who has bought into the idea that football is football; not Catholic, not Protestant, not political, not a colour, not creed. I'd like to impart the highest honour of Respect on to those who have realised that change was, and still is, needed. Who will continue to sing the most vibrant, passionate and at times hilarious football chants from home and away stands all across Europe, without use of bigotry or political rhetoric to support their football team.

"Why? Because every one of them are – in my eyes – brave ambassadors for a different way forward."

# IAN WOODS (SENIOR SKY NEWS REPORTER, INTERNATIONAL GLOBETROTTER AND NORTHERN IRELAND SUPPORTER)

"During my time as 'Sky's man in America' I was probably the only person dancing in the streets of New Orleans after Hurricane Katrina. That was down to David Healy.

"I was based in Washington and had made arrangements to watch the Northern Ireland/England game in October 2005 in a sports bar there. Then Katrina devastated New Orleans and Sky sent me south to cover the story, which quickly became the biggest one around the world. Between being so busy, the time difference and the horror of what I was seeing, the match went out of my head. When I phoned the office in London towards the end of the day all the conversation, quite naturally, was about the story.

"Almost as an afterthought I enquired about the Northern Ireland/England result and was told it had finished 1-0. I expressed the view that Northern Ireland had done well to hold a star-studded England side to a single goal defeat. It was then I was told that the 1-0 was a victory for Northern Ireland, courtesy of David Healy's goal.

"Maybe it was relief at getting some good news after covering such an awful story all day, but my joy was uncontained. I was literally dancing around the place, screaming with joy. Any Northern Ireland win is always sweet and a cause for celebration. But never had victory tasted sweeter than it did that day in 'the Big Easy'.

"I was still working in the States when George Best died. When I heard the news my mind immediately went back to when, as a seven-year-old, I went to Windsor Park to see Northern Ireland play England. There were almost 60,000 shoehorned into Windsor Park and we were standing on the terraces opposite the main stand. Down at the railway end of the ground to my left, Gordon Banks, World Cup winner and iconic England goalkeeper casually threw the ball in the air to fly-kick it upfield.

"Bestie was in like flint and in a flash had flicked it over the bemused keeper's head, raced past him and headed the ball into the empty net with Banks in hot, but hopeless pursuit. When the referee disallowed the goal for alleged ungentlemanly conduct the crowd was devastated. None more so than one forlorn seven-year-old who, it has to be admitted, did not have the greatest of views of the incident in the midst of thousands of heaving, swaying adult bodies.

"To add insult to injury, when the incident was shown that evening on television it was quite clear that George had been hard done by, and the 'goal' should have been allowed to stand. I can still remember Brian Moore, who was hosting the programme, holding up a copy of the local sports paper *Ireland's Saturday Night* which had the headline '*We Wuz Robbed!*'

"In recent years I have become friendly with Gerry Armstrong who now works at Sky. He was the hero of the 1982 World Cup in Spain, scoring that memorable goal that knocked out the hosts that night in Valencia.

"That evening I had just finished my 'A' levels and had gathered to watch the match and have a barbecue with some mates at one of their houses. The food was served

*Ian Woods (far right) with fellow fans and a typically happy-go-lucky Lawrie Sanchez.*

during half time in the match, and I was first in the queue. Having gathered up my bits and pieces I headed back into the house and the match had just re-started. Gerry scored very early in the second half and I was the only one in the room to see it. Hearing my whoops of delight the others rushed into the room, to see me jumping up and down, food strewn in my wake.

"I was also at the game against Israel in Belfast which secured qualification for that World Cup tournament. Once again Gerry popped in the vital goal and sparked massive celebrations. After the game I rushed from Windsor to the Ulster Hall to see The Kinks in concert. Ray Davies has never sounded better singing 'Lola'. A perfect end to a perfect day."

*Eamonn Holmes practises his goal keeping.*

# Eamonn Holmes (Broadcasting icon, who describes cars as his weakness and football as his passion)

"For people of my generation the magic of the Northern Ireland football team begins with George Best. Seeing him and the likes of Derek Dougan in that distinctive dark green shirt with the celtic cross on it holds special memories. We might not have had the best team in the world, but with George on board we had the best player – in all senses of the word.

"But then how could we have had the best team? How could Northern Ireland with a population of around 1.5 million compete with countries which had 60 million or more to draw on? What *we* had instead was George Best. He gave us the magic. He was always mentioned in the same breath as Pele, Beckenbauer, Cruyff and the all-time greats of the game. George was special. He always had the crowd on the edge of their seats, and then there was that great murmur of anticipation from the crowd when he got the ball.

"One of the most vivid memories I have was the day he challenged Gordon Banks, who had thrown the ball in the air to kick it downfield. George flicked it over his head, ran round him and stuck it in the net. The referee, for reasons best known to himself, disallowed the goal. We wuz robbed, ref! Then to add insult to injury, Allan Clarke of Leeds scampered through from an offside position to grab the only goal of the game played on 15 May 1971. How I would love to see a statue of George somewhere in the centre of Belfast wearing that Northern Ireland shirt. It would not only be a fitting tribute but also a magnet for tourists.

"One of the greatest things about being a Northern Ireland fan is that feeling you get that they always seem to manage to punch above their weight. A good example of that was the 1982 World Cup in Spain when the team made the quarter finals, repeating the achievement of the 1958 squad in Sweden. A proud record.

"The great thing about that tournament was that the Northern Ireland supporters were able to go to Spain in considerable numbers, and were welcomed everywhere as they just wanted to enjoy themselves, have a holiday and watch the football.

"None more so than 'Yer Man'. He was local comedian Sammy Mackie, who appeared everywhere in his Northern Ireland scarf, duncher and had a huge green and white rosette on his jacket. He had released a single 'I'm Yer Man', which was doing better then than any of the other World Cup songs at that time. I was working at UTV at the time. I filmed Sammy in action and we featured his song. I suppose a whole new career in making pop videos beckoned but I decided to stick to what I knew.

"The thing about playing for Northern Ireland, even in these days of overpaid Premiership prima donnas, is that they still play for the shirt. It would seem that the players still consider it a privilege to play for their country, which is not always the case elsewhere.

"When you look at Northern Ireland today, it is about territories being less defined. The change in attitudes is there for all to see and that has been reflected on the terraces at Windsor Park. There is now a feelgood factor amongst the supporters, which has come through on programmes on 5 Live and Sky News, and I am obviously pleased to be able to report it.

"The next thing which will happen is a change in the dynamic of the Northern Ireland team, which will inevitably start to reflect the multi-cultural nature of the population. The people from Africa, China and other parts of Europe who live in Northern Ireland will ultimately become part of the football team."

# JIM MAGILTON (IPSWICH TOWN MANAGER, BBC PUNDIT AND FORMER NORTHERN IRELAND INTERNATIONAL)

*Jim Magilton.*

"I will never forget my first cap. It was a game against Poland at Windsor Park in February 1991. All my family were there and I felt so proud.

"Some people had been given me a bit of stick before the game. They said that being from the heart of west Belfast the crowd would get on to me. Quite the reverse happened. They were very supportive from Day One. In fact I would have to say that the Northern Ireland supporters were always good to me. They seemed to appreciate the way I played. They knew I was a football man who wanted to get the ball down and pass it, and they liked that. It may also have helped, mind you, that I scored on my debut, which turned out to be a 3-1 win over the Poles.

"Playing at Windsor that night fulfilled an ambition that I had harboured for some years. The special atmosphere of that football ground is something that has to be sampled firsthand to be appreciated properly. I remember when Michael O'Neill and I were schoolboy internationals we were invited to be ball boys at a Northern Ireland game.

"We were young teenagers at the time, but the first thing that hit me when we were waiting in the dressing room area was the smell. That waft of wintergreen that you only get in football changing rooms. Suddenly the door opened and there they were. The Northern Ireland team. Pat Jennings, Martin O'Neill and all the big names. All my heroes.

> " ...MICHAEL AND I WERE TOLD TO STAND IN FRONT OF THE KOP. IT WAS JUST A CAULDRON OF NOISE AND TWO YOUNG BOYS IMMEDIATELY WANTED A PIECE OF THAT ACTION. "

"As we came out from the back of the south stand the noise began. Once we hit the pitch it was deafening. Michael and I were told to stand in front of the Kop. It was just a cauldron of noise and two young boys immediately wanted a piece of that action. It was a dream to come back to Windsor as a Northern Ireland player, which I was later proud to do and to go on to win 52 caps.

"During that time I came to realise that Windsor was just as special a place to play football as any of the much vaunted grounds around the world. When the noise starts and the crowd get behind the team the place really begins rocking. It lifts the players no end, and they and the crowd feed off one another.

"People should never underestimate the impact of the fans. They are sometimes described as the 'Twelfth Man' and I can understand why people would suggest that. David Healy and the present day team are lucky because the ground is sold out every time they play. They deserve that, mind you, because they have achieved some fabulous results.

"When I played it was often not completely sold out. But the crowd always made its presence felt and I always loved them for that. There has always been a special relationship between the Northern Ireland team and the fans anyhow.

"When I first got into the team the fans would often come round to the team hotel at away games for a post-match drink and mingle freely with the players. The senior pros at the time like Alan McDonald, Colin Clarke and Nigel Worthington assured the new boys that this was the way it was after Northern Ireland games.

"A special relationship exists between the management, players, the fans and the press. That is traditional, and all parties respect the fact that certain lines are never crossed. It is based on respect, I suppose.

"People talk about the sectarian chants and songs when I was a player. But to be honest, once the game starts you are too focused to notice. I have to say that we find ourselves in a more preferable situation these days. There is a feelgood factor around Windsor. People are going along to the games as a family, and that has to be good news for everyone.

"It is also great to see the ever increasing number of Northern Ireland tops being worn around Belfast and beyond. Often when I am travelling over I see fellow travellers bedecked in their Northern Ireland gear. The excitement around the Northern Ireland team these days is great to see. The fans have played a major role in creating that, by changing the complexion of Windsor Park.

"But the IFA deserve plaudits too. They have tried to help the fans achieve their goals in this regard. They have involved them in various committees, they have listened to their ideas and worked to make things better for everyone."

# PATRICK KIELTY (COMEDIAN AND FOOTBALL NUT)

"Most Northern Ireland supporters feel that the only place to have been on 5 September 2005 was Windsor Park. It was the night David Healy scored *that goal*. The night Northern Ireland beat England.

"I have to disagree. From my perspective the best place in the world to be that night as a fan of Northern Ireland was in my local pub in London. Here I was 500 yards from Stamford Bridge. Just about as far behind enemy lines as it was possible to be, listening to the England supporters and having to stomach that belief they have that victory was a mere formality.

"You know that Ian Wright sort of attitude – that they are so far ahead of the other nations that they can't be bothered to play the Home International Championship any more against Scotland, Wales and Northern Ireland. This was the sort of attitude that we get all the time, but that week it was particularly bad. Deep down you are thinking 'I'd love to chin these guys' – but you daren't put your head above the parapet.

"You think we are obsessed in Northern Ireland with flags and emblems. Well let me tell you that every time England play some neighbours of mine put out the English flag of St George so being on the opposite side can be a lonely existence.

*'A Night in November' star Patrick Kielty.*

"However some months before Northern Ireland played England in Belfast I had gone to Twickenham. Lawrence Dallaglio got me tickets for the England/Ireland Six Nations game. Ireland won that day, and despite being surrounded by England supporters you end up feeling that you have to cheer for your team. I did and Ireland won. So when the Northern Ireland game started all bets were off. It was time to stand up and be counted, even in Morrison's pub, near Chelsea's ground in the heart of English territory.

"When David Healy scored I was ecstatic, which put me in a reasonably elite group in that particular pub. Then I got that dread that comes over you. Have we had our moment? Are they going to come back and chin us now? But we held our ground. The final score flashed up on the screen: Northern Ireland 1 – England 0. We had won. Deep joy.

"The England supporters slunk out of the pub speechless. The nation that gave the game to the world had been beaten by a bunch of Paddies. Watching them head home in silence was the best moment I had experienced since I came to live in London. It was the best feeling in the world.

"I know the atmosphere in Belfast was brilliant, but for those of us who lived in London it was extra special because we have to live day and daily with the mantra ringing in our ears that 'England are the best team in the world'. I felt like marching down Piccadilly with my hard hat and my sash swinging a shillelagh!

"Now some people will find that sort of euphoria hard to square with me appearing in *A Night in November,* and I find that very disappointing. The play was exactly that – a piece of drama. It was an historical piece from fifteen years ago. Part of it was set at a football match between Northern Ireland and the Republic, but it was not about football or the Northern Ireland supporters per se. It was about sectarianism. It was about Kenneth. It was about working class people with middle class aspirations. It was also the first time I had appeared on a stage speaking someone else's words.

"The one thing it was not was a slight on the Northern Ireland supporters. It was a piece of historical drama. When I came to do it at the Grand Opera House I suddenly found myself on *Talkback* defending it with Marie Jones who wrote the play.

"One guy came on and said that the sectarianism had been eradicated and the play should have been changed to reflect that. I explained that as it was an historical piece that was not possible, as it had to mirror the events and mood of the time. He contended it was a bit archaic and I suggested that perhaps this was a good thing, in that it showed it was of its time and wasn't it encouraging how things had moved on. I then pointed out that history was history. I mean you can't rewrite *The Sound of Music* and take the Nazis out because the war is over.

"Just as the England team can't rewrite history and erase that 1-0 defeat at Windsor Park."

## MAY MCFETTRIDGE (NORTHERN IRELAND'S FAVOURITE HOUSEWIFE)

"The change in atmosphere at Windsor Park has been remarkable. There were times in the past when the sectarianism was impossible to listen to. It would have put people off going to the matches, but not now. The fans seem to go to the games to have fun and enjoy the occasion. There are new songs like 'We're Not Brazil, We're Northern Ireland' and of course 'The Bouncy'.

"When I think of Northern Ireland games, one night which sticks out in my mind was when the Republic came to play at Windsor. Vauxhall were one of the sponsors and about a fortnight before the game… now hold on was it a fortnight? No let's say two weeks, a man with a swanky accent phoned me and says:

'Miss McFettridge we would like you to take penalties at George Dunlop, the former Northern Ireland goalkeeper before the game. Afterwards there will be drinks and something to eat in the viewing lounge.'

"Happy days, I thought. A few wee vodka and sodas after a wee kick-about.

"So before the game May was out on the pitch in her football kit, playing 'keepy-uppy' with the ball at the railway end of the ground. Eventually I flicked it into the air and as it dropped I volleyed it. God guided it into the top corner of the net.

The roar from the crowd could have been heard in Dublin. Then more cheers, when I took five penalties and scored them all. To be honest having to face an attractive woman like myself put Geordie Dunlop off. His mind was on other things.

Then I went up to the viewing lounge and the Vauxhall man says to me: 'Vodka and soda, Miss McFettridge?'

'Just a vodka thanks,' I told him. 'I'm not hungry.'

"To be honest I think all the excitement, the crowd cheering and everything had made me lose my appetite. Then the match started and it was 1-1, and time was running out. Then one of the fellas who was watching the match shouts over to me to get my kit back on.

'You look more likely to score than anybody out there,' he says.

"Everybody laughed but I took a reddener."

*May McFettridge*

69

# DANA (ROSEMARY BROWN SCALLON, EUROVISION WINNER, FORMER MEP AND DERRY'S BEST-KNOWN FEMALE WHO RECORDED THE 1982 WORLD CUP SONG WITH NI TEAM)

"When I was in Belfast to launch my book at Stormont in the autumn of 2007 I bumped into Martin O'Neill and Pat Jennings. They were part of the Northern Ireland squad that I recorded the official World Cup song with.

"It was called 'Yer Man', and the boys joined in the recording session with great gusto. Some of them were a bit embarrassed mind you, but no more than I would have been if someone had asked me to put on a Northern Ireland jersey and try to play football. Let's just say that as a footballer I would have made them seem like great singers! But our stint in the studio was a bit of fun in the run up to the boys leaving for Spain, and the serious business of playing Honduras, Yugoslavia and the host nation.

"While it may have been a bit of a laugh in the recording studio, when we appeared to perform the number on *Top of the Pops* some of the guys were quite nervous. Quite understandable, given the millions of people who were looking in. But they carried it off fine with the shyer members of the squad standing at the back, trying to pretend they weren't there!

"When the team went off to Spain I headed for Blackpool, where I was doing summer season with Little and Large. One of the proudest moments of my life came when I heard the song being sung on *Match of the Day* by the supporters.

"On the night Northern Ireland played Spain in Valencia I was on stage at the Opera House in Blackpool as usual. I was hugely disappointed to find that there was no television backstage to allow me to keep in touch with the match. There were no mobile phones in those days, so no opportunity to ring or text anyone to get the latest score. Unknown to me the boys backstage had managed to get the result, but they did not relay this to me while I was on stage.

*Dana.*

"I came off and was called back for an encore. Suddenly the dancers rushed on and lifted me up on to their shoulders. Little and Large then appeared and announced that Northern Ireland had beaten Spain with Gerry Armstrong's goal. The band immediately struck up 'Yer Man' and the whole company and 3000 people in the audience, who by now were on their feet, belted out the song.

"It was a moment I'll never forget, as the people in the theatre jumped up and down while the dancers continued to bounce me up and down on their shoulders. At the end everybody cheered. The audience were delighted, even though very few of them would have been from Northern Ireland. It was just one of those moments I will never forget. Very special. Very emotional.

"The fact that the team did so well in Spain gave everyone a boost, in what were dark days back in the early 1980s. But then football has a very important role to play in that it gives a focus to many young people. It provides an outlet for many young kids who would otherwise just be hanging around the streets.

"I was thrilled when the Northern Ireland supporters received their award. They have done so much to move things away from a sectarian situation to one where going to watch the team is a fun night out for families. The fact that they have managed to do this, and also invested a lot of time and effort into various charity projects deserves recognition.

"I always say we have the best people in the world here, if they just get half a chance."

# DENISE WATSON (BBC AWARD-WINNING SPORTS JOURNALIST AND NORTHERN IRELAND FAN)

"In 1982 I was ten years old but like the rest of our wee country I remember Espana '82 very clearly. And that's unusual as I'm the daughter of a Rugby player/coach who had lived and breathed *that* sport above football. But even my Dad was moved by the exploits of eleven men as opposed to fifteen – especially Martin O'Neill, Gerry Armstrong and Billy Bingham in Spain.

"The funny thing is, it's not Gerry Armstrong's legendary goal against Spain which I remember as *my* highlight. *(Sorry about that Gerry!)* For some reason I was enchanted by the tall, athletic centre forward Billy Hamilton. He may not have had the flair or awesome skills of a Van Basten or Lineker, but he was in the right place when it mattered. His two goals against Austria were particularly memorable. And I loved the genuine enthusiasm of his celebrations: 'How about that then boys?'

"I'm very lucky to have met Billy on several occasions in my career, as he has worked alongside us at the BBC on the recent international matches as a studio pundit and radio summariser. And he's pretty clued in there too! What's even more pleasing is that he has never possessed any cockiness or arrogance which is often associated with the Premier League footballers of this generation.

"That whole team – which was moulded by the charismatic Billy Bingham – played for the shirt. There didn't seem to be any big

*Billy Hamilton.*

egos. They were all so proud to play for their country and be a part of a winning team. Well, that's my impression of them anyway.

"Moving forward in time, one of my major disappointments was that I wasn't present at Windsor Park the night that NI beat England and the night that David Healy became a national treasure. I was over seven months pregnant with my lovely wee girl Sam, and the excitement would've been too much! I guess David Healy became my 'Billy Hamilton' figure after that night.

"This may seem strange but – despite working in Sport at the BBC since 1996 – I only met David face-to-face in May 2008 at the Northern Ireland Football Writers Awards, where he was honoured as our International Player of the Year.

"I really wanted to say hello but was so nervous. Crazy eh? Anyway – I went across to his table and said: 'Hi David. I'm Denise from the BBC. I just want to say well done on the award.'

"And he said: 'Thanks. Yeah, I know who you are. Nice to meet you.'

"I was absolutely thrilled. I had to pinch myself. How lucky we are to have someone so talented yet so modest play for Northern Ireland."

*Denise Watson.*

# MARIE JONES (PLAYWRIGHT AND NORTHERN IRELAND SUPPORTER)

*Marie Jones in the Grand Opera House, Belfast.*

"My eldest son Darren has been going to Northern Ireland games for over fifteen years. After I had written the play *A Night In November* he was unimpressed, and suggested that I went along again to see how things had changed.

"Despite his reservations about the play he had stopped going (to games) himself for a while when the sectarian thing got too horrible. He felt I had a duty to do that. By this stage my youngest son David was about seven and he wanted to go so, I went to a game with Spain at Windsor Park.

"I was due back at the Lyric where the play was running for a 'question and answer' session on stage after the show, so I had intended to leave early in the second half. But I got caught up in the atmosphere, the singing, the drama – I mean it was like the best theatre I had ever been at. They had been on a bad run, but that night against a Spanish side filled with major players they got a 0-0 draw.

"I stayed to the end and I thought as I rushed over to the Lyric what a fantastic experience it had been. So from that wonderful

72

piece of live theatre I went over to the real theatre, and all I could talk about was Northern Ireland drawing with Spain.

"I couldn't stop talking to the audience there about the theatrics of live football. They had just been watching *A Night in November*, and I was able to tell them about all the changes there had been to the atmosphere at Northern Ireland games. Changes that had been brought about by the fans themselves. Nobody else could have done it except them, and that needs to be remembered.

"Since then I go to all the Northern Ireland games at Windsor, and I have been to away matches in Poland and Denmark. I love it and I was so disappointed that we failed to make Euro 2008, because I was planning to go over there. The craic would have been ninety.

"I used to love it when they sang: *'Oh Sammy, Sammy. Sammy, Sammy, Sammy, Sammy McIlroy.'* Then he left and they started *'Lawrie Lawrie give us a smile'* at Lawrie Sanchez, who was such a morose character with a long face.

"But that is what is so great about it. It's the wit, the joy, the pain, the singing. I go into the Kop with the boys, and having three sons it is so good to be able to go and do something with them that we all enjoy so much.

"I remember walking home one night after a match, and this guy starts singing 'Away In A Manger' and I'm thinking what is he at, that is a Christmas carol. Then he gets to *'The stars in the bright sky look down on…Healy'* everybody roared with laughter and suddenly it all made sense. What wit!

"Then there were the '1298' T-shirts when the team went that number of minutes without scoring a goal. We were suddenly the best in the world at something: all right it was not scoring goals, but let's celebrate anyhow.

"It soon spawned that joke when Saddam Hussein appeared on TV, coming out of the bunker he had been hiding in. The pictures were flashed around the world of him saying something to his captors. Immediately the word was out that he said to them: 'Have Northern Ireland managed to score a goal yet?' That sort of humour sets the fans here apart from any others. I thought that was brilliant, and the humour and I suppose the camaraderie of a football match is special. I am no expert but I now feel that I know a lot more about the game than I did when I first started to go regularly.

"In 2007 I got a lot of stick when *A Night in November* went back on in the Opera House. Most of it came through the 'Our Wee Country' website, and my son Darren rang me and said 'Mummy, you had better get on and defend yourself.'

"All the stuff that was on there was about 'Why is this play on?', 'It's showing us all up in a bad light' and so on. I had to go on and explain that the play was a piece of history, and it has played all over the world, because people don't look at it as being about football or the Northern Ireland supporters. It is about sectarianism, racism and someone changing their intransigent views. The bit where it focuses on football lasts for about five minutes. It is a man's journey in his head.

"Now there were some brilliant supporters who went on to say to the critics of the play 'Dry your eyes and let it be'. But when I looked into it more carefully it became clear that it was not a mass of people saying these things, just the same four or five people again and again.

"Some people were saying on the web 'Don't listen to these people. Come into Hunter's for a drink'. So I went into Hunter's pub, to be greeted by a bunch of fans singing *'Shite in November'* which we all had a good laugh about.

"My oldest son goes with the Carrick fans. They are the ones with the drums and the bugles. They make a day of it, and it has become a fun occasion. A great day out. The Northern Ireland supporters enjoy themselves win or lose, unlike a lot of other fans. That is their secret, and David Healy is their hero. I was delighted when he got his MBE. Despite his success there is a lovely humility about him, he is just a real genuine guy and I am delighted for him."

# SARA BOOTH (NORTHERN IRELAND WOMEN'S TEAM AND DEVELOPMENT OFFICER FOR THE LADIES' GAME AT THE IFA)

*Hazelwood College girls team with former pupil and international Sara Booth (far right) and teacher Sabrina Campbell.*

"I began playing football at the age of five and have been playing ever since. At primary school near Ballyshannon in Donegal I was stuck in nets by the other kids. I had caught the fever.

"At the age of seven I went to Whitehouse Primary School after we moved to Belfast. I wanted to play there, but found there were no girls allowed. Knowing I would pester her to death my Mum badgered the school principal into letting me join in with the boys. He reluctantly agreed, but once they realised I could play it was fine.

"I ended up as captain but that cut no ice when I went to Hazelwood College. The 'No Girls' thing reared its ugly head again. Once more Mum persuaded the headmaster to give me a go. Once more I became a regular.

"At the age of 15 I discovered Post Office Ladies' who were the leading women's team of the time. I joined them and within a year I had become a full Northern Ireland international.

"Back in 1992 things were rather different. We played in hand-me-down kits, but what we lacked in equipment and so on was made up for by the enthusiasm of the women who played. They loved the game and at PO Ladies nobody more so than Sandie Shaw. She had reached the veteran stage but was one of the best readers of the game I have ever come across.

"I played beside her at the centre of defence, a mixture of youth and experience. She was my eyes and I became her legs. She could spot danger a mile off and taught me so

*Girls play five-a-side in half-time during the international against Spain at Windsor Park.*

much. Another memorable player from that time was Rhoda Cassidy, who was to become the first woman here to qualify as a UEFA 'A' Licence coach. She was a striker in the Mark Hughes mould. What a player.

"All the girls who played for Northern Ireland were avid fans of the senior team. We used to go along to Windsor to the matches, and since I've been working at the IFA all the girls always come to me looking for tickets – which seem to be more difficult to get by the match.

"The upsurge of interest in the ladies' game since I began working at the IFA has been incredible. It has also been like that in other areas too. You just have to look at the way business has increased in the IFA shop, and think about the number of Northern Ireland shirts you see people wearing to know that things have changed for the better. The fans have obviously played their part in this too. The Amalgamation

has worked hard at it, and the sectarianism which used to put so many people off going to games has gone. I think this change in mindset reflects the way things have changed in society here as a whole.

"For me the great thing about the fans is their enthusiasm. I am thinking here about times when I have had some of our young players taking part in five-a-side games at half time during internationals at Windsor Park.

"The fans gave them a great welcome, watched the games intently and cheered the goals that were scored as loudly as if they had won a cup final. This meant an awful lot to the young girls who were playing. It was a thrill for them just to get on the pitch where Northern Ireland played. To get cheers and support like that from the crowd made it even more special. I felt so proud of the fans, and so pleased for the players.

*Northern Ireland women's team at the Algarve cup.*

"Before we headed off to Portugal for the Algarve Cup in 2005 some members of the senior team took part in a crossbar challenge at half time in a Northern Ireland game. When one of the girls hit the bar the crowd went bananas, another proud moment.

"Imagine the delight there was for our Under-19 team to play at Windsor Park against France in 2003. It was great for me to be part of the backroom staff, but a genuine thrill for the girls to play at the home of Northern Ireland international football.

"The girls all recognise how important it is for the game as a whole here that Northern Ireland is a successful team. The highs of recent years have been brilliant for the game here. A successful Northern Ireland team percolates down to everyone who plays the game here. They generate the cash which supports the other teams, and helps the IFA's 'Football for All' strategy to continue.

"I have been proud to be part of the development of the women's game here. But as the game gets more and more popular we need more funding and more people to get involved in coaching and administration at grassroots level. That is obviously something which is for the government and the IFA to address. We have made progress and while it is great to feel that you have helped to make a difference there also has to be recognition that the job is far from finished. We need a new national stadium which can generate some of the cash needed to take things to the next level."

*Green and White Girls in Spain.*

*Northern Ireland Women's Team with Manager Alfie Wylie before their match against Czech Republic at Coleraine Showgrounds in May 2007.*

# 'Punters with Typewriters!'

As the immediate past chairman of the Northern Ireland Football Writers Association I am in virtual daily contact with the journalists who have told the story of the Northern Ireland team down the years.

Their memories of that task are many and varied. I remember during the campaign to qualify for the World Cup in Spain in 1982 the now retired and usually ice-cool Bill Clark of the *Sunday Mirror* becoming unusually jumpy in the press box. Northern Ireland were playing Scotland at Windsor Park and the game was still scoreless midway through the second half.

Mal Donaghy made an unusually sloppy back pass but Pat Jennings spared his blushes with a sprint to pick up the ball. As the big man clutched it in one of those shovel-like hands of his, Bill, normally quiet as a church mouse, shrieked: "Mal! What on earth are you doing playing fast and loose with my Spanish holiday?"

Bill's outburst merely served to underline the tension that there was amongst the press corps at that time. They all had a burning desire to see Northern Ireland succeed. This led one Scottish journalist to describe his Northern Ireland colleagues as "punters with typewriters". The irony in the remark was totally lost on him because the lads from Scotland tend to be positively blinkered when it comes to their team.

The local press always try to give praise and criticism where appropriate. But in my time in journalism I have never known them to adopt the brutal viciousness of the English press. When England was beaten by David Healy's goal in Belfast the reaction of the visiting press was a mixture of disbelief, churlishness and anger.

*Reporter Adrian Logan can't hide his delight.*

I must say that it never ceases to amaze me that the English media always have their team as one of the favourites for any competition. In truth their record makes the logic of that difficult to comprehend. We still hear a lot about 1966 but never that it was over forty years ago!

It must be said that down the years, with one notable and recent exception, relations between the local press and the Northern Ireland manager and players has always been excellent. That is certainly the case with Nigel Worthington at the helm. But then being a distinguished former Northern Ireland player meant that he knew the score from Day One. Nigel has stated quite unequivocally elsewhere in this book his affection and appreciation for the 'Green And White Army'. They in turn know that he is 100 per cent committed, both to the job and to trying to get his team to get the ball down and play.

One man who has kept a watchful eye over events regarding the Northern Ireland team in recent years is Mark McIntosh, who took over from Bill Clark at the *Sunday Mirror*. Mark had developed a reputation for pulling no punches. He always asks the question that needs to be asked, which tended to annoy a certain Mr Sanchez who appeared to like everything to be written with his spin on it.

But Mark, who is of a similar age to many of the current Northern Ireland squad, always does his job in a professional way and is respected for that. His appreciation of the Northern Ireland fans is evident from his contribution which follows.

# Mark McIntosh (Sunday Mirror)

"Forget the colour of the Dutch or the noise of the Brazilians, the Green and White Army steal the show wherever they go. On many international trips, the highlight has been to get yourself to whatever square the Northern Ireland fans have taken over.

"A great memory was from the last game of the World Cup 2006 qualifiers in Vienna. The fans had gathered beside a large picturesque apartment block, conveniently facing the golden arches of McDonalds and staggering distance from more off-licenses than you knew what to do with.

"Despite some people buying non-alcoholic beer without their knowledge, the party was in full swing, when an elderly woman appeared on a balcony on the top floor of the apartments. Within seconds she was spotted by the Northern Ireland fans who, quick as a flash, burst into a chorus of 'God Save the Queen'. Whether or not the newest member of the Green and White Army had a clue of the reference to the Palace-like surroundings didn't matter. She loved it, the fans loved it and even the locals managed a chuckle.

"Another fantastic memory comes from the night David Healy broke the international goal-scoring record in Tobago. Our Caribbean chums turned the night into a bit of a festival and before kick-off they introduced an athlete to run around the track with the Trinidad and Tobago flag.

"One Norn Iron fan decided he wanted a piece of the action and with flag draped around him, he scaled a small wall and sprinted to catch up. Within seconds he was gasping for air in the Caribbean drizzle, but there was time for both athletes to pose for a few photographs. But there are memories like that from every trip and long may that continue."

As Mark has indicated the quick wit of the fans is legendary. Mind you some of the press boys have their moments too. None more so than Jackie Fullerton. As he walked through a square in Liechtenstein which was a sea of green and white he was approached by half a dozen fans. They were bedecked in Northern Ireland kit, their faces painted in the colours of their team and green wigs atop their heads.

"Over for the match lads?" quipped Jackie.

*Northern Ireland journalist, Mark McIntosh.*

# Jackie Fullerton *(BBC Northern Ireland)*

Ever the housewives' choice on the BBC, many tend to forget that Fullerton actually began his television career at UTV. When Northern Ireland made it two World Cups on the bounce under Billy Bingham by qualifying for Mexico in 1986, Jackie was duly despatched from Havelock House to cover events.

"I remember about two hours before Northern Ireland's opening game with Algeria at the Estadio Tres de Marzo, Guadalajara filming a group of about forty fans who had agreed to sing for the camera ahead of some being interviewed.

"The musical end of things was wrapped very quickly and just as I am about to interview the first guy he says to me: 'Is this for home Jackie?'

'What do you think?' I replied.

'Ah well in that case you'll have to scrub me from the whole thing. I shouldn't be here. I'm doing the double.'

"So we had to begin all over again filming the singing, but before we did I asked were there any others who were signing on the dole and wished to be excluded? Another five sheepishly dropped out and we filmed the others. Then came the interview.

"My first question to one of the fans was 'How did you get here?' Before he could speak a voice from the back chipped in 'By canoe'. We all dissolved in laughter on the spot, and I had to start again. But that sense of humour is what I love about the Northern Ireland fans. They make you proud to be from here.

*Jackie Fullerton with former international Ian Stewart.*

"During that World Cup Pat Jennings won the last of his 119 international caps, in the final game against Brazil on the day of his 41st birthday. The Northern Ireland fans freely mingled with the Brazilians. There was no segregation necessary because they don't let themselves or their country down, as so often happens with the England fans. The Brazilians always want to party, carnival as they call it, and the Northern Ireland fans are exactly the same. Everybody enjoyed the day.

"But then even in defeat the Northern Ireland fans just keep singing. Never has that struck me more than during the 4-0 defeat by England at Old Trafford in March 2005. Despite being outnumbered their voices could be heard resounding around 'The Theatre of Dreams'. They had to stay on afterwards until the England fans cleared and they just kept singing.

"The England team came out for a warm-down and David Beckham led them over to where the Northern Ireland fans were, and he and his team applauded them. That was a nice moment and it underlined that the fans are determined to enjoy every occasion and make the most of every visit to every country.

"One of the fans I have got to know down the years is Roy 'Big Skin' Martin. We were in Ukraine and on the Saturday morning John O'Neill, the former Northern Ireland defender who was summarising, Joel Taggart and myself took a stroll to get something to eat.

"We noticed as we passed the town hall that a civil wedding ceremony was going on. A few of the Northern Ireland fans were hanging around watching. A few hours later I noticed 'Big Skin' enter the ground complete with suit, shirt and tie. Apparently he had met the happy couple the previous evening and got invited to their big day! 'Good day so far

Skin?' I asked him. 'Great wedding. Great craic and a great cake as well Jackie,' came the reply.

"But that's the Northern Ireland fans. Jim Rainey and Michael Boyd have done a tremendous job trying to eradicate any sectarianism. It's not perfect, but then very few things are in this world."

Another journo who shares Jackie's waspish sense of humour is Stephen Looney from *Sunday World*. Never one to shy away from dealing with contentious issues, he and members of the Green and White Army have been at loggerheads at times. However, the supporters respect the fact that he is passionate about Northern Ireland football and always calls it as he sees it. His respect for them is mutual as it's clear from what he has to say in the next few paragraphs.

# Stephen Looney (Sunday World)

"Northern Ireland fans deserve tremendous credit for taking the bull by the horns and addressing the sectarian element of the crowd in the wake of Neil Lennon's retirement. The Green And White Army took it upon themselves to drown out the 'party songs' with their own upbeat chants and support, and successfully marginalised the idiots to the point of almost total eradication."

"My clearest recollection of the new, fun support following Norn Iron was out in the Ukraine back in 2003, when the Northern Ireland supporters were in their element. Jim Rainey played conductor with his loudhailer, urging his cohorts onto the 'Party Train' and bringing real humour to the terraces. Because Northern Ireland were enduring their infamous barren goalscoring spell perhaps it was gallows humour, but the boys were having a ball and it was uplifting to listen to.

"The Green and White Army grew in numbers and, for me personally, the pinnacle of their achievements came

when they travelled to the Millennium Stadium in force for Northern Ireland's World Cup qualifier on 8 September 2004. Around 5000 fans travelled to Wales to get behind their team, determined to give a good account of themselves in this mini Battle of Britain. Despite being outnumbered by close to 70,000 home fans, the Northern Ireland support outdid their hosts when it came to singing before, during and after the game, which ended in a 2-2 draw.

"A nation noted for their singing was humbled in their own backyard, and I will never forget the embarrassed PA announcer, who desperately tried to lift the Welsh support before kick-off. I cherish the moment of triumph when I heard the announcer admit defeat by crying, 'Come on Wales, you're being outsung in your own stadium!'

"A magical moment for the best fans in Europe."

*Stephen Looney*

81

# Orla Bannon *(The Mirror)*

*Orla Bannon*

"There is no remote outpost of Europe too bleak or too unpalatable for the Northern Ireland away fan. He (or she) is never put off by distance, time zone or the state of the local economy. The away trips in recent years have included some pretty remote destinations. Armenia, Azerbaijan, Estonia, Leichenstein... not exactly tourist hot spots, yet the Green and White Army got there in their droves.

"The resourcefulness of these supporters is incredible. Like the time Northern Ireland played Finland in a friendly in Helsinki in August 2006. The hard-core remembered how much fun they'd had in Estonia two years earlier on the cheap beer. Rather than pay £6 a pint in Helsinki, hundreds of them lived it up in Tallinn for a couple of nights before taking a 30-minute hover-craft ride across the Baltics into Helsinki on match day.

"One of the most bizarre journeys was to Yerevan, the capital of Armenia. The place was cold and unfriendly and all the time Mount Ararat, where Noah is reputed to have built his Ark, cast a dark shadow of gloom over the whole town. In need of some light relief one scallywag, let's call him 'Noah', stole a bust of some revered eastern bloc leader out of a nightclub and put a Northern Ireland scarf around its neck.

"The next morning he woke up to find his arm wrapped tightly around the metal object of his desire, on the pillow next to him. When he honourably tried to bring it back the following evening, the nightclub owners tried to get him arrested but 'Noah' somehow escaped.

"Can't remember what the result was from that particular trip. Might have been two-by-two..."

*Michael Duff in action against Latvia in Riga.*

# Jim Gracey (Sports Editor Sunday Life and bon viveur)

'What's football got to do with supporters?' a former IFA suit sniffily retorted when I raised the concerns of a ticketless group who'd travelled for days to see Our Wee Country in some far-flung Eastern European outpost. We weren't going that well but that didn't deter the loyal band from travelling.

"The suits at the time were so out of step with the rank and file supporters, they'd told their hosts no more than a handful would turn up. And when they did, they could fend for themselves, was the attitude. Besides, organising tickets for them would mean five minutes away from the free bar.

'But what about the supporters?' I pleaded, as the tired and ticketless stood like dogs at dinnertime outside the reception room door. And that's when they were given their pedigree, as perceived by that then IFA grandee, who, thankfully, is no longer there.

"A few phone calls later, myself and a few media mates had them sorted, the lads saw the game and, of course, we lost. But they still deemed their journey necessary. That was over 20 years ago. There was no need for gratitude, even at the time, yet to this day those lads remember the episode and remind me of it every time our paths cross in airport lounges and late night foreign bars.

"Supporters never forget a good turn. I never forget a bad one, and that dismissive comment has stayed with me, summing up, as it did, all that was wrong with the IFA of old and the contempt in which they held those who indirectly sponsored their junketing.

"Happily, things have changed at Windsor Avenue. But not with the supporters. They still travel far and wide in support of our boys, only in greater numbers, which is good. And their resourcefulness in finding their way to the remotest places would do a military Task Force proud. The fans' presence was always appreciated by the players. Today, in sharp contrast to 20 years ago, they are also valued by the IFA, who now know where their bread is buttered.

"I saw evidence of that a few years ago in Spain when I happened upon a disconsolate 1st Shankill contingent, marooned in Benidorm by a wildcat bus strike, unable to get to the game in Albacete, four hours away.

"A quick phone call to the team hotel, another two hours in the opposite direction in Valencia, saw Jim Boyce, the man they called the 'People's President', hop in a taxi out to the airport where he commandeered a tourist bus, and despatched it to Benidorm so the Shankill boys would see the match. Which we lost. Again.

"I don't know what it is with the Shankill club and buses, because that reminds me of another escapade in Greece a few years earlier, when the boys hired a bus from a bloke in a bar to take them to a match in next door Yugoslavia. All went well until they were stopped at the Greek border.

'You cannot leave the country in this bus!' barked an official.

*Jim Gracey*

*Windsor Park faithful with a lone Spanish player.*

'Why? We've got our passports and visas and here's the insurance,' explained the lads. 'So why not?'

'Because it is stolen!'

"Don't ask me how but they got to the game. You can guess the result. If Northern Ireland played on the moon, the little green men would be our supporters. They are the salt of the earth and they look out for one another like family. And its great for me, a 40-year veteran, to see new generations swell the ranks of the Green and White Army.

"No matter what the result, I've had great fun in foreign parts with pals like 'Winkie' Rea and 'Big Skin' Martin of the Shankill Club. And great rows over the Maze with my good friends Jim Rainey and Gary McAllister of the Amalgamation. But we never fell out. That is how it is with the band of brothers who follow Northern Ireland. Every one a valued member, whatever their view on a great game of many splendoured opinions.

"What's football got to do with supporters? Just about everything really. If it wasn't for the supporters, there'd be no suits in first class seats. And, unlike them – and us meejah types – they always pay their way!"

# Dr. Malcolm Brodie MBE – The Doyen

*From left: Alex Steele, Amalgamation of Northern Ireland Supporters' Clubs, Dickie Best, father of George, with Dr. Malcolm Brodie.*

When Malcolm Brodie began covering Northern Ireland matches just after the Second World War he was neither a doctor nor an MBE. But he was to go on to become the jewel in the crown of football journalism in the Province.

Forever associated with the Belfast Telegraph he has seen the highs and lows for the Northern Ireland team both at home and abroad. He continues to cover their games to this day, and wherever football is played he is known simply as 'The Doyen'.

"Over the years NI supporters could be described as extremely loyal and totally passionate. They had their dark spots on occasions, particularly the Neil Lennon issue at Windsor Park, but generally speaking I have found the fans from this part of the world to be primarily interested in football.

"In recent seasons the establishment of the 'Green and White Army', the improved form of the team, inspired by that 1-0 victory over England and the goals of David Healy has made them into people who are purely interested in football.

"They dream of Northern Ireland reaching the final of a major tournament – either the World Cup or the European Championship. The magic created by Sweden '58 and Spain and Mexico in the 1980s lives on."

"Sweden 1958 was a football tournament organised by football people, an entirely different era from that of today. There were not the constraints of commercialisation and massive and overpowering security, and the basic concentration of the fans concerned what happened on the pitch.

For me, 1958 was the last of those type of tournaments. Northern Ireland battled through to the quarter-final stage having qualified after the memorable win over Italy in Belfast. The fans travelled to Sweden, but in nothing like the numbers which follow the team today. They got there by motor scooters, even in some cases by pushbike, having travelled across on coal boats and freight ships.

"Supporters wandered around the grounds of the team hotel mingling with the players. Some fans even set up a tent in the grounds and it became known as 'Dave's Café'. They would give us tea and even in the morning set down a fry for you. Indeed some of the players, instead of having breakfast in the hotel, used to go out there for a fry, served up by a guy called Mickey McColgan.

"In Spain the supporters were more used to foreign travel than they had been 24 years previously in Sweden. The NI camp, despite the security and so on, was still 'open house'. The team did well too. We had some world class players, and you need to have that sort of quality for these tournaments. The climax was that night in Valencia when Gerry Armstrong scored that goal which proved decisive in the 1-0 win over Spain.

"Gerry is one of the great characters of Northern Ireland football, strong, skilful, effervescent, the most kindly of men, who has been dining out on that goal ever since. But that was the great uplift for Northern Ireland fans. It showed we had a team which was no longer the Cinderella of world football.

*The fans make their feelings known.*

"We measured up again with qualification for Mexico in 1986 and unfortunately some fans thought it was always going to be like that. They thought it was just a matter of time before we won the World Cup. There has been a huge dose of reality since then, but to be fair to the fans their support never really waned. Since David Healy's scoring feats became a phenomenon of the Northern Ireland team things have been on the up again.

"I have to say that I have been very impressed by the conduct of the supporters, both at home and abroad and by the work done by the Amalgamation of Northern Ireland Supporters' Clubs. I was presented with an award from them at their last annual dinner which I appreciated. I have been impressed too with their organisational ability, and for the responsibility they take for the conduct of their members. They are a credit to this country.

"I also found that the amount of charitable work they have done without ever asking for any plaudits was quite remarkable. I think the Amalgamation must take credit for the input they have given to the game here. Managers from Billy Bingham up to Nigel Worthington consider them to be the Northern Ireland team's 'Twelfth Man'.

*A sea of green in the Alex Russell Stand.*

"That, of course, was also the case in days gone by, when George Best and before him Peter Doherty played. They were Northern Ireland's top players ever, and the murmur of expectancy from the fans when they got the ball showed they were every bit as passionate as the fans of today.

"But then don't forget we were getting capacity crowds of 58,000 back in those days at Windsor Park. One thing that has never changed about the Northern Ireland supporters over the years is that they have always appreciated class, skill and technique. George Best was having the same impact around the world then as Cristiano Ronaldo is for Manchester United today. That was special for the fans because he was one of their own.

"Let me be frank. Down the years I have had a love/hate relationship with the supporters, especially when I was Sports Editor of the *Belfast Telegraph,* and they perhaps disagreed with something I had written. However I must say that I am pleased to have earned their respect and they have mine as well. I'm proud to be part of them when we are on tour, proud

that they have been officially recognized by UEFA with the Brussels Supporters award.

"Tribute has to be paid also to Michael Boyd at the IFA Community Relations Division who has worked extremely hard at ensuring everything goes right at games, that bigotry has been kicked out and that all the '-isms' vanish. He has done this job against a background of great difficulty, and made Windsor Park an area where anyone can go.

"The fans reserve the right to challenge the football authorities when they feel that they are getting a raw deal. This has applied particularly over the farce of the so-called 'Maze International Stadium'.

"That is why – and I have advocated this from day one of the debate as to where Northern Ireland international matches should be played – Windsor Park should be refurbished and continue to be used as the home of the Northern Ireland team. It has an atmosphere and it has a heritage, and you cannot transfer that from one site to another."

*Members of the Lambeg Cricket Club / NI Supporters' Club in Gran Canaria*

# THE FUTURE

# Green and White Superheroes

Dr. Mark Elliott is Northern Ireland's best-known sports psychologist. He has worked with former world boxing champion Brian Magee, Lisburn Distillery FC and emerging international surf star Ronan Oertzen, amongst others. Here he presents a professional perspective on the changing face of the Green and White Army.

This is TM's story – a case study in change and a psychological perspective on the sea change within Northern Ireland supporters.

'TM' is Northern Ireland's Mr Football. However, he has had a highly charged and challenging life. Moulded as he was by the so-called Troubles, sculpted as he was by his 'wee country's' toxic tribalism, TM's belief system hardened through childhood, with his feelings and actions following suit.

Self-righteousness played tag with denial, excitement, hatred and fear. TM became a troubled young man, spiralling downwards towards rock bottom, and acting out within a literal vicious circle. The prognosis was not good, especially as TM's environment maintained much of his behaviour. Both TM and his environment had to change. Indeed, his environment was like a feeder club to his unhealthy, prejudiced psyche.

Northern Ireland was torn apart by social conflict, a conflagration that bled into all life domains, both internal and external. Attitudes curdled, and unhealthy emotions and behaviours moved through communities on the back of a malignant mistral. The ill-wind swept through all social arenas, from home to school, through churches, pubs and clubs; it gusted also into TM's territory.

*The team celebrates the amazing win over England.*

Conflict or ethnic tension infects all in its path. That great euphemism for the battleground, Sport, was ripe for the expression of tribal identities and factional mindsets. Windsor Park, TM's Manor, was never going to be immune. TM felt at home at Windsor, and in a mirroring of society, 'visitors' weren't welcome. Rock bottom was reached!

While TM remained wedded to his Troubles-tainted identity for many years, he has recently undergone the most remarkable of transitions. Change is difficult, and TM deserves credit, moving as he has beyond many a sceptic's expectations.

But he had to change. TM's transformation reflected socio-political development. As the political situation contaminated TM's formative years, it had now became a role model persuading and 'permitting' him to drop his ego-defences and to grow into a well-balanced, inclusive and exuberant 'individual'.

Excuses had become fewer and redundant. In light of the new Northern Ireland and of the prevailing *zeitgeist*, TM stood up, and conceded that he needed help, that he needed to change. TM was listened to, encouraged to build bridges with his neighbours and to move forward positively. Will TM relapse? Well, when under stress we can all revert to our old destructive habits. But, if peace prevails, the mirror is clear.

And who is TM? He is the Northern Ireland team's Twelfth Man! 'He' is the men, women, boys and girls who follow Northern Ireland. TM is now the best in Europe. The transition is complete!

# Where do we go from here?

There is no doubt that the future for Northern Ireland internationally is inextricably linked to where they play. A new stadium appears to be generally accepted as the best way forward. Mind you getting consensus as to where it should be is another matter. Some fans believe the best solution would be to give Windsor Park a makeover and increase its capacity to 25,000 to 30,000.

Shaun Schofield, who has written a book about his time supporting Northern Ireland, has a view that is echoed by many members of the Green and White Army after just missing out on qualification for Euro 2008.

"Away from the pitch I just hope everyone can stop arguing and let us have a new stadium, as it is a national scandal that at present there are fans being locked out of matches and can't see their team play, because of the limited capacity of the current ground.

"On the field I think we are still very much on an upward curve: it was unfortunate what happened in Iceland and Latvia, which in the end prevented us from qualifying for Euro 2008. But hopefully Nigel Worthington and the team have learned from that, which I think they have, judging by the way we ended the qualifying campaign. Let's just hope we can now win a few games and end up in South Africa in 2010."

That would also be the hope of Howard Wells. But unlike those on the terraces the man charged with charting the IFA's course through the current difficult waters has a raft of things to address. He is trying to maximise the earning potential of the Northern Ireland brand off the pitch, support what Nigel Worthington is trying to achieve on it, and at the same time grapple with improving the domestic game.

"The Sky deal has been important because we needed to get profile for Northern Ireland football pan-UK and beyond," reasons Wells. "While the stadium situation remains unresolved we need to find other ways of generating income. We've maximised the TV deal and will improve the merchandising deals before the end of the year.

"That leaves ticket sales as our only other means of generating income. At present we take over a season what Chelsea generate in one match. The reality is that we need a new stadium yesterday or we face having to dismantle all the infrastructure we have put in place, and that will hit the game here at every level right down to grassroots."

*The Northern Ireland Squad and staff prior to the match against Georgia at Windsor Park.*

Wells has been careful to keep the fans informed about what is happening right down the line. But then his five-year plan, which spells out clearly what needs to be done.

"It has six key components," explains Wells. "It's a marker for the future and can be implemented whether I'm here or not."

Ambitious plans are afoot to introduce IFA TV which will be available via the website (www.irishfa.com). IFA Telecom and IFA Finance providing credit cards and even mortgages, will follow.

"The days when the IFA could exist on the revenue from home games have long since gone," admits Geoff Wilson. "We need to find other ways to generate revenue. The money

that is brought in is all re-invested in the game here. We are actively involved in local football, grassroots, the women's game and football for people with learning difficulties. Our strap line is 'IFA Bringing Communities Together' and we are committed to that now and into the future."

On the playing front: what are Nigel Worthington's plans as Northern Ireland attempt to qualify for the 2010 World Cup in South Africa?

"We have a difficult task in our 2010 World Cup qualifying games, especially with Poland and Czech Republic in our group. But I am confident our fighting spirit will shine through, and my main concern is that we improve our record away from Windsor Park.

*The fans say what they think.*

"We know the fans will be behind us all the way, and with our blend of youth and experience I hope we will give them plenty to cheer about. Northern Ireland is always at its best when we operate as a team. The supporters are very much part of that team as far as I am concerned."

That is music to the ears of Jim Rainey who is a leading member of the Amalgamation of NI Supporters clubs. He has been supporting his country since the year before the first World Cup adventure to Sweden in 1958. So how does he see the immediate future?

"We obviously need to get the stadium issue sorted out. Everyone knows the Amalgamation has always been against the Maze and in favour of a new stadium being built in Belfast. I feel, as do the majority of our members, that this is the only logical decision.

"As for the team, I think we still have some good players in the side, but it all depends what is coming up through the ranks. Whether or not we can carry on the momentum from the last Euro qualifying series to the forthcoming World Cup games remains to be seen though."

Listening to all concerned it would appear that the Green and White Army is on the march. At the time of writing the Maze stadium scheme seems dead in the water. All that is required is for someone in government to officially administer the last rites. Once that is officially confirmed the problem would appear to be a lack of any plan B. Concrete proposals (no pun intended) for a new build in Belfast are presently non-existent, which could possibly put a refurbished Windsor Park back on the agenda.

In the current vacuum one thing is absolutely certain. The longer the prevarication about the stadium goes on, the more all the interested parties look like those who marched behind the Grand Old Duke of York.

# Thanks...

I would just like to say thank you to everyone who co-operated so freely with me in writing this book.

I am grateful to the IFA whose chief executive and staff were all very accommodating. The members of the Green and White Army also played a blinder as did many others too numerous to mention.

Particular thanks to my colleagues from the Northern Ireland Football Writers Association whose continued support to me in sickness and in health typifies what a great bunch of people they are.

I must also mention Marshall Gillespie whose attention to detail, ability to twin incidents with dates and times and genuine love of Northern Ireland football is in a different class.

Jean Brown once again proved that to be a great editor you don't need to be built like a brick outhouse, crack a whip or yell a lot. Her patience and support at a time when she had much more important people to think about than me was humbling.

Finally to Suzanne, Daniel and James who put up with my idiosyncratic ways and continue to fill our home with laughter.

Ivan Martin

# Acknowledgements...

The publisher would like to thank the following for permission to reproduce work in copyright:

pp 5, 21 (left) © IFA. Photograph by Spike Hill
pp 6, 24, 26 and 96 © IFA
p 21 © Profile Publishing
p 22 © IFA. Photograph by Stephen Hamilton
p 23 © IFA. Photograph by Gary Hancock
p 24 © Sperrinview Special School
p 25 © Belfast Deaf United
p 33 (left) and p 71 (centre) © *Lancashire Evening Post*
pp 33 (right), 40, 41, 70 (right) and 95 © Appletree Press
pp 35, 42 and 60 © ASP
p 36 © Stuart Glencross
p 39 (right) © Emerald Music
p 48 © South of England NI Supporters' Club
p 50 © Shaun Schofield
p 53 © www.ourweecountry.co.uk
p 57 © Stiff Little Fingers
p 58 © George Jones
p 59 © Catherine McGinley
p 63 © Ian Woods
p 64 © Eamonn Holmes
p 66 © Jim Magilton
p 68 © Patrick Kielty
p 69 © John Linehan
p 70 (left) © Dana
p 71 (right) © BBC
p 72 © Marie Jones
pp 74 and 76 © IFA. Photographs by Sara Booth
p 81 © *Sunday World*
p 82 (top) © *The Mirror*
p 83 © *Sunday Life*
pp 86, 87 and 94 © www.oneteaminireland.co.uk

The publisher would also like to thank Lee Purcell for his kind assistance with memorabilia.